For Sherry & Bernie,
With Best Wishes!

LETTERS
from the
ATTIC

LETTERS
from the
ATTIC

Dusty Thoughts and Remembrances

CHUCK BROWN

HENNEPIN HOUSE

Copyright © 2015 by Chuck Brown

All rights reserved. No part of this publication may be reproduced, stored in a retrieval system, or transmitted, in any form or by any means, electronic, mechanical, photocopying, recording, or otherwise, without the prior written permission of the author.

ISBN-13: 978-0-692-34560-3
LCCN: 2015937255

Cover Design by Alan Pranke
Typeset by B. Cook

Printed in the United States of America

ALSO BY CHUCK BROWN
Barn Dance
The Lake Hayes Regatta
Dunn Days

In loving memory of
Ben & Clara
Charles & Fritzie

ACKNOWLEDGMENTS

Thanks to my editor, Cathy Broberg, for once more working her magic, and my cousin, Bobbie, for her help with rounding up pictures. Credit to my sister, Judy, for her usual enthusiastic support and also for pestering me until I got around to taking on this project. And as always, thanks to my wife, Pat, for her help on this book and for all that she brings to my life.

CONTENTS

Prologue xiii

Chapter 1: Boxcar Children 1

Chapter 2: Up to the Lake 7

Chapter 3: At Sea 15

Chapter 4: Outhouses and Other Houses 23

Chapter 5: Jumpers and Speakers 31

Chapter 6: Querencia 37

Chapter 7: Methodists at the Folies Bergere 43

Chapter 8: Golf 53

Chapter 9: Rock-ribbed Republicans 59

Chapter 10: Halftime 67

Chapter 11: Curmudgeons and Carpet 73

Chapter 12: Food, Glorious Food! 79

Chapter 13: What's in a Name? 87

Chapter 14: Beauty 93

Chapter 15: Getting Grandpa's Goat 99

Chapter 16: Kodak Moments 105

Chapter 17: The Only Catholic on the Lake 111

Chapter 18: Nebraska Wordsmiths 117

Chapter 19: Heroes 125

Epilogue 135

PROLOGUE

In 2005 my wife, Pat, and I moved into a house in Olivia, Minnesota, that my grandparents built in 1955. At the time of construction they were already in their sixties and they lived there just ten years before both dying in 1965. During the intervening years my parents occupied the house, together until my father's death in 2000, then my mother alone until 2005.

The point I'm making, right here at the very start, is that I am the third generation of my family to live in this house and that only my family has ever lived there. Not much of a point, really; not the sort of historic chain of events likely to move someone to read a book, much less write one. And this sort of multi-generational occupation of the same house was a good deal more common in days gone by when we were a more agrarian and less mobile people. The family farm comes to mind where one could spend a childhood doing chores and helping out, then grow into adulthood, marry and have children. Meanwhile, the parents, now grandparents, move to a smaller bedroom down the hall from whence they offer advice, much of it unheeded. This is the Waltons model, though I mention it with the risk that an ever-growing number will ask, "Who the hell are the Waltons?"

My family didn't follow the Waltons model. We didn't overlap and we weren't farmers, though each of us—my grandfather, my father, and I—took a turn at managing the same business, just as we would take a turn at living in the same house. Nor can I argue that we were closer or better off or a more loving family for having lived in the same house. If there is a difference it is this: more stuff accumulates in the house from one generation to the next.

In the course of modern American life, we move often and for many reasons: graduation, new job, marriage, divorce, retirement, fleeing winter, fleeing debt, and so on. Each move is a catharsis, a chance at new life, and also a chance to throw out all the junk that has accumulated for no good reason. Indeed, whoever moves into the house you've just vacated has every expectation that you will have taken all your stuff with you, but there is no such expectation if those moving in are the next generation of your family. Under those circumstances the junk tends to stay, especially so if the house in question has a large attic.

Our attic is not only large, it's also accessible, and accessibility is important. If the only way to get stuff up there is by hoisting it through a ceiling hatch while teetering on a stepladder, then the accumulation will be smaller. Our attic has no such chokepoint, as there's a perfectly good stairway leading up from the garage, the end result being that we moved into a house with two generations' worth of stuff already up there. There wasn't room for any of our stuff. It was full!

I credit my parents, Charles and Fritzie, for most of the hoard. They lived there longest, after all, and they also approached attic-filling with practiced teamwork. My father was a saver, a packrat, a child of the Great Depression who was loath to throw anything away. Couple that with my mother's passion for shopping, and in no time at all you've got a full attic. The inventory was long and varied, and revealed a special fondness for old rusty bedsprings together with a commensurate number of musty mattresses. There were odd pieces of furniture that no one wanted. There was an outboard motor. And then there was old carpeting, roll after roll of it. That Dad saved old carpeting wasn't surprising—lots of people do—but he also rolled up the old carpet padding and hauled that up to the attic too. Why he saved carpet padding I cannot say. I can only speculate that he was conducting scientific research to determine what happens to old carpet padding when it's stored in this manner. He didn't live to see the result of the study; he left that to me, and I can factually state that the stuff crumbles to powder when dragged down a stairway.

Filling the space between all these treasures was an almost unending collection of life's debris, some of it boxed, some of it lying about loose, all of it patiently waiting for me. In the months after we moved in, I came to be on a first-name basis with the folks at the county landfill as I hauled pickup load after pickup load down there, but I was thankful that Dad spared me one task: disposing of his *Sports Illustrated* collection.

Dad liked sports. He subscribed to *Sports Illustrated* for over forty years, and his fondness for the magazine was confirmed by his refusal to throw them out once he finished reading them. Instead, he lovingly placed each issue in his special *Sports Illustrated* repository, said repository also functioning as the attic stairway. Great endeavors usually start at the bottom and proceed upward, and so it was with Dad's repository. He started on the bottom step, stacking each week's issue until the pile was a foot or so high before moving up to the second step. This was all part of Dad's plan to reread them once he finally retired, but when his ascending archive reached the top step, he had a change of heart. He may have concluded that the fire marshal would frown on so large a hoard of combustible material, or perhaps the ever-narrowing stairway compromised his ability to haul more stuff up to the attic, or he may have simply come up with a better plan for his golden years. Whatever his reason, he did finally clear out the collection.

Today my attic stands in sharp contrast to its cluttered past, but that is not to say it's empty. I admit to storing some of our stuff up there, though we try to adhere to Attic Rule No. 1, which states that for anything going up, something else must come down. Nor should any of this suggest that everything I found in the attic was junk, that nothing

A HOUSE WITH A ROOMY, ACCESSIBLE ATTIC.

was of value. There remain a few worthy pieces of furniture, notably a couple carved headboards, and a fair amount of family memorabilia to be retained for posterity. Included in the memorabilia was a certain packet of letters, which are, at last, the point of all this.

In May of 1948 my grandmother, Clara, sailed from Montreal on the *Empress of Canada*, a 20,000-ton liner bound for Liverpool. Her journey was noted in the *Olivia Times-Journal* with the following comment: "Mrs. B. A. Brown of Olivia is leaving today for an interesting trip that will take her to several countries in Europe. She will be accompanied by her brother-in-law and sister, Dr. and Mrs. L. P. Ganfield of St. Paul. The party will leave from Montreal, Canada by boat to England on May 22. They will tour places of interest in England, France, Belgium, Denmark, and in Norway they will visit relatives for several days. They plan to return on June 30."

It was to be the trip of a lifetime, a journey that a few years earlier would have been made impossible by World War II. My grandfather, Ben, chose not to go along. That may have been because it was planting season, a busy time in the canning business, or perhaps he simply didn't feel the pull of the motherland, of Norway, from which my grandmother's parents had emigrated. Whatever Ben's reason for staying home, they weren't revealed in the letters I found, but so much more was.

During the course of the trip, my grandparents wrote often and long. Each had much to say to the other, thoughts limited only by the available surface on a sheet of paper. They started at the very top and wrote from edge to edge, all the way to the bottom on both sides, often squeezing final thoughts into a cornered sentence. Their letters spoke of faraway places, and of Olivia, Minnesota, a place so familiar to me, yet faraway when seen through their eyes across the span of years. Their letters spoke of family and everyday occurrences, of hopes and longings, of tender thoughts and irritations, but mostly they spoke of two people very much in love and unaccustomed to long separation.

Before starting this book I paused to wonder if, by revealing personal letters, I might be committing an egregious breech of privacy, and my own family's privacy at that. In the end I decided that while it may well be a breech, it is nonetheless an acceptable one. For one thing, both Ben and Clara are long dead. For another, their letters disclose no dark family secrets or scandals—a deficiency that usually argues *against* publication in today's tell-all publishing world.

Mostly I decided to go ahead simply because I thought the letters were worth sharing. They're well written in the sense that people used to invest a good deal of time and thought in letter writing, a practice largely lost in today's sterile, electronic missives, carelessly sent through e-mail and social media. The letters also convey nostalgic warmth, which admittedly could be another argument against publication, as folks nostalgic about places like Olivia are likely to represent a small target audience, but so be it. And finally, as a rather lazy writer, I must confess that taking on a project where someone else has already done a good deal of the writing held a certain appeal.

There are nineteen letters in all, ten from Clara and nine from Ben. I will present them chronologically, and follow each one with a brief essay from me. In some cases my comments will be restricted to the content of their letters; in others, I will use their letters as a springboard into family or Olivia history. I may climb on a soapbox or two. The letters are faithfully reproduced without editing or abridgement. I kept their abbreviations and colloquial spellings. In rare instances I added punctuation with you, the reader, in mind. Otherwise they are solely the thoughts and words of Ben and Clara.

CHAPTER 1

BOXCAR CHILDREN

Fri. eve –Montreal, Canada

My Dearest Ben,

So far, so good—except that I miss you dreadfully—even thot I'd like to take the train back home to you when we got here this aft. It just doesn't seem right to be traveling without you—and to be going so far away from you. I hated so to leave you yesterday—guess it's a good thing you left in such a hurry else I'd probably have wept on your shoulder—was so close to it all morning, thinking of leaving you.

We had an uneventful trip so far. Didn't spend but a short time up in the Vista Dome between the cities—it was warm up there and I could see enuf in my seat. No one else got on in that car so we had plenty of room. We arrived on time in Chicago—went directly to the central station, checked our luggage, and then walked down Michigan Ave over to State and back to the Stevens where we had dinner in the coffee shop. I tried to get the clasp on my bag fixed, but it would take a while, so couldn't get it done. It should be O.K. tho. We left Chicago at 8:45, and after sitting in the lounge a short time went to bed. We had connecting bedrooms which made it nice. It was so hot in Chicago, but the train was air conditioned so we were very comfortable. Had a pretty good sleep, tho I woke up a number of times. Customs wasn't bad—the inspector stopped at the door this morning—asked if it was personal luggage. Bertha said yes, and that was all.

I don't seem to be doing too well with this pen—but have decided I'd better use a lighter touch. [Clara refers to ink blotches.]

We got into Toronto this morning at 8:30, so had time to take a little walk outside before our train left at 9:15. There is a Mr. & Mrs. Jensen from Mpls who were on our train last night and today who are sailing with us tomorrow, but are going to Sweden. We rode in the chair car today, but the train wasn't too nice—nor too bad. The wife of one of the executives of the C. P. Railroad sat near us and kept us entertained and informed. She really was most attractive and very nice. We've had sunny weather till this noon when it clouded over, and it is a drizzly evening now. They've had a lot of rain all week here. We got in about six o'clock—came to this hotel, a big old one, but new furniture and nice room—old fashioned bathroom. After we checked in we went up the street a ways to a nice little lunch room and ate our supper, then we walked over to the depot—a block from here—where we will be leaving from when we come back to inquire about return reservations. Now we are back in our rooms—which are connecting. I like that as I don't feel so alone. They have twin beds, and I have a big double bed—lots of room for you. I so wish you were here.

Am going to bed pretty quick. Will probably go on board early, as we can do that anytime after eight o'clock.

Take good care of yourself, my dearest. I love you so, and am missing you so all the time. Don't forget to love me and miss me too. Am remembering the goodnight kiss for tonight. And do try to take it easy. Am always thinking of you. Goodnight my dearest—all my love from your own wife.

Clara

Clara took up her pen again the very next day so her second letter follows here. Hereafter their letters will alternate chapter by chapter.

Empress of Canada, Sat. PM

My Dearest Ben,

One last word to you while I am still on this side. We are on our way, but can leave mail at Quebec, so thot I'd drop you a note to tell you I love you so much and am missing you such a lot.

Our boat sailed on time, and I felt you were thinking of me then. It had been cloudy all morning. We came down to the boat soon after we had breakfast. Didn't take long to go thru customs, but had to stand in line quite a while to be checked onto the ship. We got settled in our stateroom and then went up on deck to see the leave taking. There were lots of folks down to see us go, and we had paper streamers to throw over to the crowd below. Just as we pulled out the sun came out—a good omen for us—tho it didn't stay out too long. We stayed on deck quite a while watching the skyline—we are close to shore, the river isn't very wide here—so of course we hardly know we are moving. We had a very good lunch—just got thru now. We were late, so sat at the second table. We are assigned to the 1st table tho, so after this will be eating early. We also are assigned to table 31 where we will be eating the rest of the trip—today everyone ate any place.

It is a bit chilly—some women with fur coats look very comfortable. Leo hasn't even a topcoat, but it will probably warm up if the sun comes out.

Had a good rest last night—went to bed after I wrote you and really slept sound. Decided to call Virginia before I went to bed—she was surprised to hear my voice, but seemed glad to hear mine. She was alone—said Ira is so busy, he is working so hard and gone a lot. She is working in a building just across the park from the hotel where we stayed. Says she loves Montreal.

Guess there isn't more to tell you now. Hope you are taking good care of yourself. Give my love to the family. Am beginning to count the days till I come back to you. I love you so much and wish so you were here.

All my love,

Clara

Clara's description of the departure from Montreal offers quite a contrast to today's travel experience. The leave-taking was an event, a celebration, with passengers throwing streamers to the crowd gathered on the dock to bid them bon voyage. She mentions going through customs almost as an afterthought. There was none of the drudgery of airport security, no removing shoes and belts, no emptying pockets, no separating oneself from one's fluids. Roomy staterooms sound like a wonderful alternative to the cramped accommodations found in coach on a jetliner. Even travel by sea is remarkably different today. Clara embarked on an ocean liner; she took a sea voyage with the idea of being delivered to some faraway port. Today's nautically inclined don't go on sea voyages. They take a cruise on a cruise ship, which entails a week or so of shopping by day and gluttony by night, then being dropped back at the place from whence they started.

It was no surprise that Clara opted to take her sea voyage with Bertha, as they were close, even for sisters, a closeness due in part to having lost both of their parents at an early age. Bonds forged in difficult times are often stronger than those that form in happy times.

Johan and Christine Corneliussen emigrated from Norway in the latter years of the nineteenth century, eventually ending up in Alta, Iowa, where they acquired farmland and started a family. Bertha was born in 1886, followed by Oscar in 1889, and finally by Clara in 1892. The family would later move to a larger farm, over 300 acres, near Slayton, Minnesota. Theirs was a typical American immigrant experience, and the future was surely filled with the dreams and possibilities that have always drawn people to this country. But then the future turned suddenly bleak. Johan and Christine both died in 1905 during an influenza epidemic when Clara was thirteen, Oscar sixteen, and Bertha, now head of the family, just nineteen.

Fortunately, they weren't completely destitute—they did have farmland and some cash. Still their dreams had surely darkened, their possibilities dwindled to but a few. What could a nineteen-year-old woman with two siblings to support hope to do in rural Minnesota in 1905? The obvious answer was to get married; find a husband who could then farm the land and provide economic security. Or sell the land, move to town, and look for work in shops; possibly marry a shopkeeper. Not many other options seemed viable for a young woman in those circumstances, but then Bertha proved to be the exception to the rule, and an audacious one at that.

Bertha hatched a plan that has always struck me as a variation on the Boxcar Children story with a collegiate twist. She refused to marry for economic security alone, believing there had to be more to marriage than that. She kept the land and rented it out, but instead of looking for shop work in town, she boldly packed up her brother and sister and moved to St. Paul, Minnesota, whereupon she bought a house, then promptly enrolled at Hamline University.

Very few men went on to college in those days, and far fewer women, so Bertha's actions were quite extraordinary even without her circumstances. Her risk paid off. At Hamline she would meet Leo Ganfield who became, not necessarily in order of importance, a dentist and the love of her life.

CLARA CORNELIUSSEN AND BEN BROWN AT HAMLINE UNIVERSITY.

Oscar followed Bertha into Hamline, then a few years later, at the young age of sixteen, so did Clara. All three siblings eventually graduated. That Clara chose to follow her sister and brother into Hamline was, for me, a good thing, actually an existential thing, for it was there that she met a handsome young man from Hanley Falls, Minnesota, named Ben Brown.

CHAPTER 2

UP TO THE LAKE

Monday Morning, May 24th

Dearest Clara,

S'pose you are out on the high seas by now and enjoying the water. Certainly hope you don't get seasick. Surely hated to see you leave last Thurs. morning and have been missing you a lot. Am sure I am going to get terribly lonesome for you before you get back. After you left I started looking around the fixture stores on Washington Ave. looking for equipment for our cook shack. Didn't have too much luck but guess maybe I will be able to find something. Also shopped around and found a shirt for Bob. Almost bought a tropical worsted suit at White's but passed it up. Was pretty tired and didn't get home in time to vote, but guess they didn't need it anyway. It carried about 3 to 1, though Hector and Fairfax both voted against it.

Have been kept plenty busy and guess I will be plenty busy all week. Have to get everything ready for the close of the year so will probably be working nights this week as I can get much more work like that done when I am alone and can concentrate. Charles presented the Legion award at commencement Friday nite. I wasn't there but several have said that he did a very nice job. Guess he must be different from his dad when it comes to speechmaking. Saturday morning I drove over to Willmar and paid the taxes, and then out to the lake. Gunder and the two boys were out there so I put in the rest of the dock with their help. Didn't do much of anything else. Just loafed around. Ann came out in the afternoon so I had supper with them, so didn't have much cooking to do. About 8:30 I drove into town to the golf club party. Didn't feel much like dancing though. I did dance once with Fritzie and called a circle two step. I left early, before supper and drove back to the lake. Went to bed and slept till 9:30 Sunday morning. There was a pretty good crowd at the party and guess it didn't break up till about 1:30 or 2:00. Fritzie said they would be out to the lake about 12:00 yesterday, but they didn't show up until after 1:00. Said the car stopped on them and it took about 40 minutes to get it going again. They said Judy cried and thought they would never get to the lake. I had bacon and eggs for breakfast, however, so didn't get too hungry. Mowed the lawn after breakfast. Didn't do it all as it is getting pretty dry. Certainly had a mob around there yesterday. Pushings and Brusts came out there fairly early and were there an hour before Jacobsons arrived. Later in the day Brandts and the Scott Bunkers drove in so Jacobsons had plenty of company. They had a tent set up on their lot. About 5:00 Dan & Ida and Lois and her family drove in and were there for about an hour. Then Gordy Schultzes arrived with their kids. Guess Fritzie had arranged with them to come out for supper so we surely had a mob. The kids didn't sleep and were pretty crabby by last nite. The water was warm and the kids were playing in it. Both Judy and Chuck fell in the water, so all in all we had quite a time.

Have almost 500 miles on the car so should be able to step on it before long. Was a little disappointed in it however on gravel roads. It seems to weave around a little which isn't a comfortable feeling. Don't know whether it is out of line or the tires are too big. Am going to have it checked today for alignment.

Am going to try to get one of the Warners to get the windows into the cottage this week. Has been pretty warm and would like to be able to open it up, which I can't do with the screens nailed in at present. Doesn't seem right at the lake without you so don't know just how much time I will spend out there. They are having a mixed tournament tomorrow nite and serving ham so may go out to eat. Everything is O.K. at home but it isn't the same without you and will be missing you terribly before you get back. Had hoped to have a letter from Montreal and am still hoping. Have a good time and take care of yourself.

All my love, Ben

Ben's first letter to Clara was quite newsy and covered a lot of different subjects, so some background information is in order.

The "cook shack" for which he was seeking fixtures was a lunchroom located next to the boiler room at the back of the Olivia Canning Company. It was equipped with a refrigerator, stove, sink, and a counter long enough to accommodate a dozen or so stools. It was, in fact, a tiny restaurant that sold breakfasts, lunches, and suppers to the factory workers employed during the pack—that is, the August/September canning season. It operated for over thirty years, which is a pretty good run for any restaurant, especially one named the cook shack. I suppose when your customers are more or less captive, you don't have to lure them in with enticing names like Italian Olive Garden. Besides, the cook shack fare was closer to boiler room than Italian, though I do recall that a good selection of pie was usually on hand.

The vote Ben missed was a plebiscite to determine if a county hospital should be built in Olivia. At the time there was no hospital in town, which explains why my mother traveled to a hospital twenty-five miles away in Willmar when I was born two years earlier.

Ben was a Cadillac man, so we can be fairly certain of the brand of car when he writes of having almost 500 miles on it. His comment about being "able to step on it before long" calls to mind the time when new cars required an extensive break-in period at low speeds.

Much of his letter, though, centered on the lake, and that was fitting since the lake was a big part of Ben and Clara's lives. Indeed, going "up to the lake" is quintessential to being Minnesotan, and that particular lake property remains a cherished gathering spot for my family to this day.

The lake in question is Big Kandiyohi Lake, located some twenty miles north of Olivia. Ben and Clara bought a fifty-foot lot on its northeast shore soon after moving to Olivia. When my dad and his sister, Shirley, were little, the family would camp out there in a tent. In time, Ben would build the first building on the lot himself: an eight-foot square storage shed. Next came a two-holer outhouse attached to the shed, followed by a small garage. This construction took place over several years while the family continued to camp in a tent, somewhat reminiscent of another housing phenomenon of that era: the basement home. Mortgage loans weren't so readily available then and a new homeowner might expend all available funds just finishing the basement and the flooring above it. That flooring was then covered with tarpaper so that it might function as a roof, allowing the family to live in the basement until they could save enough to build the next story. Ben and Clara finally got their "next story" at the lake when they built a small cottage.

During the years of construction, they were also expanding their landholding. The dry, dustbowl years of the thirties saw the lake nearly dry up. At the same time the Great Depression brought widespread economic hardship, and the disappearing water and wealth caused a number of folks to simply walk away from their lake properties. Ben, with an optimistic eye to the future, bet on both the lake and the economy coming back, and he acquired two abandoned fifty-foot lots, one on either side of his original lot, simply by paying the back taxes.

So that brings us up to the state of the lake in 1948 and the years immediately following, years that formed my earliest memories of the place. The cottage was essentially a single room measuring about twenty-two feet square. A tiny kitchen along one of the side walls was separated from the rest of the room by a partition wall that did not go all the way to the ceiling. At the back of the cottage two curtains ran on wires from the partition to the outside walls, creating two nominally private sleeping spaces. The walls and ceiling were finished completely in knotty pine. The two-hole biffy out back was still in use, and there was no electricity, so nighttime lighting came with the hiss of Coleman lanterns. If it all sounds a bit rustic, then try seeing it through the eyes of a kid, and "rustic" quickly becomes "magical."

THE COTTAGE ON BIG KANDIYOHI LAKE.

And the magic only got better in the kitchen. A hand pump mounted next to the sink drew water from a well below. If the pump wasn't used for a time, its leather gaskets would dry and it would lose prime, so a jar of priming water was kept nearby. There was a wooden ice chest outside the kitchen window, the kind you put blocks of ice in, but for keeping things like milk and eggs cool there was something much niftier. One corner of the kitchen featured a hole in the floor about eighteen inches in diameter. A concrete pipe of the same diameter as the hole and lined with tin extended down from the hole, through the crawl space, and several feet into the cool earth below. A wooden cylinder, open on one side to allow access to its shelves, fit nicely down inside the pipe. The cylinder was raised and lowered by means of a rope fair-led through a pulley anchored to the ceiling, so Clara had only to pull it up, place her groceries on the shelves, then lower it into the coolness of the earth below. Okay, so maybe it wasn't a Frigidaire, but it worked, and to a kid it was total magic.

The kid sleeping space where my sister and my cousins and I slept was filled with bunk beds and cots, and in the morning from the top bunk we could peer over the partition into the kitchen below and watch Clara make pancakes for breakfast. Clara's pancakes, made from ingredients that came out of a hole in the ground—it doesn't get any better than that.

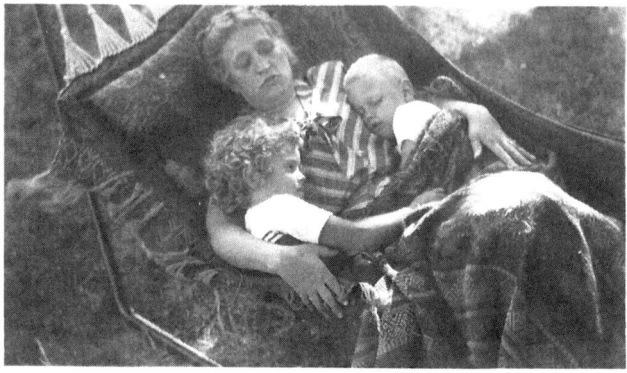

THE AUTHOR AND HIS SISTER CATCH SOME HAMMOCK
TIME WITH CLARA AT THE LAKE.

A word or two about the neighbors: Ben wrote about the mob at the lake on Sunday, many of them visiting George and Etta Jacobson next door. George was a judge and Etta was Ben's secretary and clerk at the canning company. Two doors down were Gunder and Ann Hoaglund. Gunder, known to some as Swede, was the company's plant superintendent, so it was something of an Olivia Canning Company enclave on that part of the lake.

One final footnote to Ben's letter: He mentioned wanting to bring one of the Warners out to the lake to install new windows. He was referring to the Warner Brothers who, when not making movies in Hollywood, did carpentry work in and around Olivia. Actually, they were a different set of Warner Brothers, but their work was nonetheless prized, and seven years later when Ben and Clara decided to build a house, the house where I now live, they opted for a Warner Brothers production.

CHAPTER 3

AT SEA

Empress of Canada, Friday, May 28

My Dearest Ben,

Tomorrow we land so I'll be getting a letter ready to send off to you then. Over a week now since I left you, and such a long time it seems. I have often wondered why I left my wonderful husband, to be so far away for such a long time. I do feel so lost and lonely without you and am already counting the days till I get home again. It would be much more fun to have you here to do things with—sit on the deck or walk the deck and dance. They have a good orchestra, and have dancing most every evening. I watched a little while one evening—not many dancing tho, only those who wore dinner clothes, which we haven't so far.

It's really been pretty cold on the trip, so haven't spent so much time outside as I had planned. Many women have their fur coats and look most comfortable. I put on my slacks, a couple sweaters and my coat, so keep warm enuf. Life on board ship is pretty much routine—afternoons they have movies, then tea in the lounge, then bingo or horse races and music. In the evenings concerts or dancing. Bertha and Leo always go to the movies, but I haven't gone yet. The trip has been quite smooth, but with quite a bit of rolling Sunday. They call our ship the Rolling Empress. I managed to lose my meals Sunday, but didn't feel too badly. Kept pretty much to my cabin Mon-Tues. I was so sleepy and slept most of the time. We have an airy cabin and am very comfortable there—such good beds. We've had to advance our watches one hour every night, making it an hour earlier to get up each morning, and you know me—I've had breakfast in bed every morning. Do you think I'll be spoiled? We have such a nice stewardess who brings me whatever I want. I haven't been eating very heavily—somehow I don't seem to have a very big appetite. I spend some time in the lounge and visit with different people, and much of the time I just sit, so I am really getting a good rest.

Most everyone on board is Canadian or English, and have crossed many times. We've met a few from the States—some from Minn. These English are most amazing—they say there are 40 people on board over 80 years old, and many of them traveling alone. There aren't so very many young people. There are some babies and little youngsters—which especially appeal to me. Guess I am missing my own grandchildren.

Leo seems to be enjoying the trip and is getting a good rest. He hasn't started playing any deck games tho, so must be slipping. Bertha of course has tried them, but not to any extent. We have a newspaper published every day, so keep up a bit on what is going on. We are due to arrive in Liverpool tomorrow aft—we are running about 4 hours late as we've been heading into a strong wind all the way. The folks who take the London train get off first, at 5 o'clock, the rest have to wait till later. It will seem good to get my feet on solid ground again. Am afraid I am not a good sailor. I haven't felt too badly on the trip, but haven't felt too good either—no pep—very content just to sit, so guess I am getting the rest I'd planned for.

We are so many hours ahead of you now, but I try to figure out the time and think of what you are doing. It stays light so long here—sunset about 10 o'clock last night and still twilight at midnight. Just think of the golf you could play, or the fishing you could do. I wonder if you have been out to the lake—I wished so Sunday that I were out there with you. Wonder if you've been down to Owatonna yet to play golf. First night on board at dinner the steward said that someone on shore had ordered cocktails for us. Of course Bertha said no, we wouldn't have any, but Leo and I decided to have some sherry. I tried to find out who had sent them, but the steward said he didn't know. The only one I could think of was Virginia. I'll have to call her when we come back thru.

The trip up the river was nice, and Quebec was quite a sight as we came up to the city. We stopped to take on passengers, and the city lights came on, making a very beautiful sight. All day Sunday we sailed close to the south shore. The mountains in the distance had quite a bit of snow on them, and all along the shore were little villages with their church spires.

I hope my dear that you are taking real good care of yourself and thinking of me and missing me as I miss you. I think of you so much—you are such a nice person to be thinking of, and I do love you so much.

All my love from your own Clara

P.S. We hope to see Ireland tonight.

The *Empress of Canada*'s steady progress across the Atlantic required advancing clocks one hour each night, a loss of time which in turn required Clara to have breakfast in bed each morning. Once more we can compare a sea voyage with today's travel experience, and it seems reasonable to conclude that steamship lag is far less bothersome than jet lag.

And no, the horse races aboard the Empress did not entail the likes of Secretariat galloping up and down the decks. Rather, it involved small wooden horses whose advancement along a race course was determined by the rolling of dice.

Clara, citing her modest activity, said she was getting a good rest, and a bit later she noted that Leo, too, was getting a good rest. In future letters rest will continue to be a topic for Clara, while Ben's letters will fuss about her taking it easy and not doing too much. With all this need for rest one might think that they were all on leave from a salt mine, which of course wasn't the case. As already mentioned, Leo was a dentist, and while fiddling around in people's mouths all day might become tedious, it's hardly backbreaking manual labor. Clara and Bertha were both housewives, and though housekeeping was probably harder on the back in 1948 than it is today, it wasn't the salt mine either. Still, there was good reason that Clara in particular get enough rest. She had a heart condition, the result of childhood rheumatic fever, and doctors had advised that she lead a quiet life. Ben took the advice seriously and saw to it that Clara had extra help around the house and that she didn't overexert herself. When my mother married into the family, she viewed Clara's extra help not so much as a response to health worries, but rather as a fine family tradition worthy of being carried on. Dad agreed.

The hesitancy to accept a gift of cocktails that first night on board, and then Clara and Leo's decision to have only a glass of sherry, hint at teetotalism. Not so, at least in Ben and Clara's case. In addition to being a Cadillac man and a T-bone man, Ben was also a martini man, and he and Clara regularly observed the cocktail hour. Seven years later when they built the house where I now live, Ben was sure to include a wet bar in the basement rec room. Whenever my family came for dinner, the cocktail-hour protocol went like this: the ladies would remain in the living room while Ben and my dad adjourned to the basement to make drinks. I was far short of the drinking age, but gender allowed me to come along so I can now offer this eyewitness account. Drinks were made—martinis for the men, Manhattans for the ladies—but before taking them upstairs, Ben and my dad would each knock back an extra martini. Seems that while Clara generally approved of the cocktail hour, she also counted Ben's drinks, and according to Ben's protocol the quickie in the basement was never part of the tally.

Clara mentioned the ship's newspaper that kept them up on current affairs. Luckily, Clara saved two editions so that I can now share the news of 1948 with you, dear reader. *The Empress News* was a four-page daily that included upscale ads for Paris fashions, Scotch whiskey and champagne, New York hotels and restaurants, and of course Camel cigarettes.

The lead story each day covered the growing crisis in Berlin and the early days of the Berlin Airlift: "British and United States forces have been placed on an austerity regime as a result of food and power cuts imposed by the Russian blockade in an effort to conserve food for German civilians." The next day's report sounded more optimistic: "A Berlin correspondent states that enough food for the entire German population of Berlin's western sectors will soon be available by air supplies with the imminent arrival from the United States of 40 cargo planes, each carrying seven tons and making two round trips daily. British and American planes landed over 1,000 tons of food supplies on Monday, and the air corridor was busy as the shuttle service operated at a rate of one plane every eight minutes."

Commenting from London on the Berlin situation, Winston Churchill said, "Only firmness and resolution towards the Russians, and maybe not that, can prevent a third world war." He added that the "Soviet isolation of Berlin has raised issues as grave as those at stake in Munich ten years ago."

Nor could Clara escape American politics by going to sea. There were numerous reports about the just-concluded Republican Convention and the nomination of Thomas E. Dewey for president. "A victory in November will bring to the people of our country, and I might say the people of the world, new hope, new unity and new faith in human freedom," Dewey said. Politicians have always talked that way, and I guess they always will.

Dewey received mention in no fewer than six articles while incumbent Harry Truman received only one when he was quoted as saying, "This greatest age in history is also the Machine Age." He went on to recall his boyhood when he had to milk a cow morning and night, wash dishes, and chop wood. "Now that's all done for you," Truman said. "You can just sit in bed and turn switches." With eloquence like that is it any wonder that Give 'em Hell Harry went on to beat Dewey.

One item in the papers did suggest that presidential campaigns in 1948 were not the 24/7 traveling circuses they are today: "California Governor Earl Warren left for New York to take his wife and three daughters to see some Broadway shows and other sights in the city. The 57 year old Republican choice for vice president expected to stay in New York for four days before returning to the west coast." Skip out for four days in the middle of a campaign to take in some Broadway shows with your family? Wouldn't happen today. Warren may have lost the election, but he showed the good judgment one might look for in, say, a Chief Justice of the U. S. Supreme Court.

Lest the ship's passengers grow uneasy and restless over unending reports of political shenanigans and the Soviet menace, *The Empress News* leavened its columns with lighter topics, such as this item under the headline GAILY CLAD MEN. "Los Angeles, Cal—The men's wear manufacturers of Los Angeles have announced that colors for men's autumn clothes will be gold and bronze, chartreuse and vermilion. Choicest item among new creations unveiled at a style show was a gold suede sport coat with play shoes to match." If nothing else, this tidbit serves as a reminder that words can take on new meaning over time. *Gay* and its variations is certainly such a word.

And then the Soviets were back, without the menace this time, under the headline VEGETATION ON MARS. "Leningrad— Vegetation on the planet Mars probably consists of grass-like plants and creeping bushes of greenish-blue hue, according to Professor Gavril Tikhov, Soviet founder of the science of astro-botany. In a report, Professor Tikhov said that some Martian vegetation turned brown and withered in summer while other plants preserved their color all year round."

From Leningrad it's back to Hollywood for this item: "The latest scanty bathing suits are too scanty for film star Esther Williams, a former national swimming champion. Miss Williams said today they were 'unflattering, immodest, and impractical,' and besides, she said, 'They come off in the water.'"

So there you have it: from the Soviet menace to presidential politics; from gay clothes to astro-botany to bikini mishaps. That was the lay of the land, as viewed from the sea, early in the summer of 1948. Alas, we are left to imagine what play shoes might look like.

CHAPTER 4

OUTHOUSES AND OTHER HOUSES

Wednesday, May 26th

Dearest Clara,

Not much has happened in the two days since I wrote you but on looking over the itinerary I guess I had better drop you a note today if you are to get it in Paris. Got your letter on Monday and was so glad to hear from you. I certainly hated to have you leave that morning and guess it probably was just as well that I had to get off the train rather suddenly. It's always hard for me to say goodbye—sort of have a habit of chocking up. Judy was tickled with her card and was showing me the hotel where you were staying. She was worrying yesterday as to whether you could get anything to eat on the boat.

Have had plenty to do all week. Got the windows for the cottage on Monday and thought I might as well get them fixed up so spent until midnite Monday giving them 2 coats of shellac on one side and one coat of paint on the other. Talked to Warner that nite and he said they could probably send someone out on Friday. Went out to the mixed tournament last nite for supper and then played about 4 holes, which wasn't too hot.

Guess not more than a half dozen women played, tho there was quite a crowd for supper—ham and scalloped potatoes. Came back here about 8:30 and spent a couple hours working on figures. Called Charlie this morning but he hasn't been feeling too good so wasn't very anxious to come out. Said he had to go to Chetek yesterday and took sick while there, so we had our directors meeting over the phone.

Haven't been out to the lake since Sunday and hope to get out there Friday. Doesn't seem right out there without you though so maybe I won't spend as much time there as I figured. Gunder is getting his outhouse all ready to take out. Guess they expect to have some company out there on Memorial Day and he said that Ann said she wouldn't go out there again until they had an outhouse. Jacobsons got theirs out there last week sometime. Doesn't improve the looks of the place too much.

Charles and Fritzie drove into the city today to look around for furniture. Guess Van is moving out so they hope to get Warners and the painter over there soon. Mrs. Ziesmer is staying with the kids today. Fritzie asked if it would be O.K. and I said that I wouldn't bother her and didn't think she would bother me. Was home about 10:00 and they all seemed to be O.K. She said they were used to her and they got along fine.

Saw Faye last nite at the club and she said she was going to write you. Didn't really talk to very many people as I just ate and went out to golf. Charles didn't play as they were labeling until six. They were out for supper however.

John sold the old car and it netted $1,100 so that is considerably better than trading it in. Have about 500 miles on the new car, and think I am going to like it. Haven't had too much chance to drive it, however, but guess I will use it when going to the lake to get some mileage. Awfully dry here. Lawn's drying up and the garden's not too good. Must get the tomato plants in if I ever get time. Am missing you terribly and it doesn't seem the same around here with you gone. Have a good time and don't let Leo loose in Paris. Will try to get another letter to you at Brussels.

All my love, Ben

The Charlie with whom Ben had a directors meeting over the phone was a gentleman named Charlie Fist. The Olivia Canning Company's fiscal year ended on May 31 in those days, which explains why Ben was spending so much time on the books and also why a meeting of the directors was necessary. Charlie Fist owned a food brokerage company in the Twin Cities and lived in an immodest house on Lake Minnetonka. He also owned a controlling interest in the Olivia Canning Company.

Even though Ben, then my dad, then I, continuously managed the company for some seventy-five years, none of us ever owned more than a minority share. Majority ownership changed from time to time, but it was never local, so many in Olivia simply assumed that the Browns owned the canning company outright. Since setting them straight would have involved telling them things that were none of their business, we tended to tolerate the misperception.

Speaking of tolerating things, we are left to imagine the sort of crude septic construction Gunder Hoaglund might have tolerated at the lake had Ann not insisted on an outhouse. Gunder was no lout. He was a good family man, handy around machinery, and a dependable employee, but apparently it was left to his wife to knock off the rough edges and move him along to life's finer touches, assuming an outhouse qualifies as a finer touch. Men get too much credit for civilization. Granted, they built much of it, but that was only because women told them to get their butts out of the cave and do something. Today men with chauvinistic tendencies grow wary at the ever-greater role enjoyed by women in the political and corporate worlds. Indeed, colleges are now graduating more women than men, and each year more women earn more than their husbands. I, for one, think this trend augurs well for the advancement of civilization. Gunder Hoaglund might have been skeptical, but I'm sure Ann would have agreed.

Somewhat hidden between the lines of Ben and Clara's letters so far, something that will become more apparent in future letters, is the fact that my family was staying with Ben while Clara was away. The arrangement allowed my mother to do Ben's cooking and laundry, but that wasn't the chief reason we were there. To fully understand that, we must go back nearly three years to the fall of 1945.

It was a heady time. The war was at long last over and men and women were mustering out of the service and returning home to civilian life. My dad, recently discharged from the Navy, was among them, and he had no doubts about what he wanted to do next. During the time between his graduation from college in 1939 and August 1941 when he entered Navy flight training just months ahead of Pearl Harbor, he was employed by the Hormel Company in Austin, MN, where they had developed a canned delicacy called Spam. With the war over, that experience with prestigious food products surely factored into his decision to accept a position at the Olivia Canning Company where the chief product was the equally prestigious creamed corn. Hence, there were no questions with regard to career, but housing was quite another matter.

The long war effort had sucked up nearly all that the economy could produce, making it nearly impossible to buy durable goods like cars, household appliances, and furnishings. Nor had anyone been building houses, so my folks came home in the fall of 1945 to a tight housing market, necessitating that they move in, temporarily of course, with Ben and Clara.

At the time Ben and Clara lived in the house that my family would move into again in 1955 when Ben and Clara built the house where

I now live—are you noticing a pattern here? It was a full two stories with brown stucco siding (in family lore it's known simply as the stucco house) and four bedrooms up. By the standards of the day it was a roomy house, but that roominess was soon challenged. Let me set the scene: For starters there were Ben and Clara, then my mom and dad and my sister, Judy (Mom was pregnant with me at the time). Now add to the mix Dad's sister, Shirley, and her husband, Bob, also fresh from the Navy and in need of temporary housing, along with their son, Jeff. Shirley was pregnant too, and gave birth to my cousin Barbara (known to the family as Bobbie) in January. I would follow along a month later, so if you're keeping track, we're now up to six adults, two toddlers, and two newborns. It made for quite a crowd, and by all accounts Clara was delighted and Ben went to the office a lot.

THE STUCCO HOUSE.

Eventually, Shirley and Bob went to newspapering in Nebraska, while my folks found a tiny apartment above a doctor's clinic. We lived there for several months until they were able to rent a house, a house that became available because the owners were leaving town to care for a dying relative. It took two years for the relative to die, so the owners didn't return until 1948, at which time my folks bought the house next door to the rental. That house required some painting and fixing up before we could move in, which Dad was doing, so that's why we were living with Ben at the time that Clara was on her trip, and as his letters indicate, he spent a good deal of time at the office during that occupation, too.

As noted above, we would then move into the stucco house in 1955, which was located on a tree-lined residential street with the county courthouse across the street and one block over. Being so close to county governance did nothing to detract from our sense of living in a residential area, but it did lead to a rather odd occurrence one summer night.

Across the street and down on the corner, between the stucco house and the courthouse, stood a two-story brownstone that housed the county jail. As correctional facilities go, it was fairly benign looking, and a passerby who didn't know better might have assumed it was simply a large house. It was pretty much a short-term facility; criminals actually sentenced to do time were usually sent elsewhere. The jail did, however, accommodate a certain group of, shall we say, *clients* in a manner not untypical of small towns in that era. The following description often fit these clients: male, middle-aged, single, sporadically employed, and constantly thirsty. These fellows would while away their evenings in the company of kindred souls at the municipal liquor store, sometimes called the town pump, occasionally becoming so soused as to be incapable of going home. Maybe they just forgot where home was, or maybe someone was at home who would take a dim view of their condition. Whatever the reason, the local authorities didn't want them stumbling around town all night, so it was deemed in the public interest that, should one of these fellows find his way to the jail, he be given a cell for the night where he could sleep it off.

Okay, you've got the description; now let me set the scene: it's a warm summer's eve. Crickets are chirping and the windows and doors of our stucco house are open to the night air. My mother is reading in the living room; my dad's watching the ten o'clock news in the den off the back of the living room. My mother hears the front porch screen door creak open and she looks up, dumbstruck, as a drunk weaves his way through the porch and into the living room. "Ish dish da jail?" he asks.

Mother finds her voice. "Charles!"

Dad recognizes the urgency in her tone, but the sports have just started, so instead of rushing to her aid he calls out, "What?"

Meanwhile, the drunk is gaping happily about, most likely marveling at how nicely the jail has been decorated since his last visit, not to mention the attractiveness of the jailer.

"CHARLES BROWN!" There's no mistaking Mother's tone now and Dad emerges from the den, takes the drunk by the arm, escorts him outside, and points him in the direction of the Renville County Jail. Just another Saturday night at the Brown house.

CHAPTER 5

JUMPERS AND SPEAKERS

Paris, France—May 31

My dearest Ben,

And this is Paris—and I wish you were here with me. Got in at 6 this evening. It has been drizzling all day, so the trip wasn't as nice as it might have been, but still we did enjoy it. Seems so long since I was home with you—two weeks almost gone. I still miss you so much and am counting the time till I get back to you.

To go back to last Friday when I wrote you last, we sighted Ireland about 10:30 that evening, and it was a welcome sight to everyone. Next morning we were still in sight of land and finally down the Mersey River where we docked at Liverpool at noon. We had lunch and waited on board till 4:30, until they had all our luggage off before we landed. Didn't take long to go through customs after we located our baggage. There hasn't been too much formality as yet to go thru customs. They usually ask if we just have our personal things, sometimes if we have tobacco or spirits, and once if we have firearms. They usually ask how much American and English money we have, and that has been all. We took a boat train to London and got in about 11:00 that night. It was exciting to get in, and our hotel was very nice—had a nice room and slept like a log till Bertha awakened me. We had breakfast at the hotel, then took a bus for Westminster Abbey where we attended services. Queen Mary and General Montgomery were there but we didn't know till after, so didn't see them. We walked over to take a look at the Parliament building, then took a boat trip down the Thames as far as the Tower Bridge. We saw the Tower of London, London Bridge, the old fish market, the site of Shakespeare's playhouse, and many more interesting things. As we came along we came to a man in the water who had jumped off one of the bridges, so the boat maneuvered around and finally got hold of him with a hook, then they had to take him to police headquarters. It was rather depressing, though the man was able to walk off with assistance.

After lunch we walked through Hyde Park, which was very large and lovely and filled with people. At Orators' Row in Hyde Park we listened to different fellows spouting and letting off steam. The sun came out for a little, and then it was warm, but mostly cold and cloudy—the weather has been since we left home. I had my suit and coat on and still it was cold. Went to bed rather early as I was tired and we had to get up early this morning. Bertha and Leo went for a walk, but weren't out long.

We left London a 9:20 for Dover where we took the boat for Calais. Stayed on deck and enjoyed the crossing, which wasn't much over an hour. Then we took the train for Paris. We have seen so many bombed out areas, though they are rebuilding very fast and cleaning out the rubble. We have talked to many interesting people and are really seeing lots of interest. This evening we walked up Champs Elysees as far as the Arc de Triomphe. We stopped in a French restaurant for supper and had a good meal. We have quite a time keeping track of our English and French money—we get almost 300 francs for the dollar. I still have 3 English pounds, so am not spending too much. Tomorrow we go on a couple sightseeing tours, and then on to Brussels Wednesday.

Had hoped to have a letter from you at London—am missing you so, and always wondering what you are doing. I dream of you so often, and I like that as you seem so near then. I'm wondering if Charles and Fritzie are still at home to take care of you. Will be so glad to hear from you and better yet to get home to you. I love you so.

All my love, Clara

Here's the deal: you're on the trip of a lifetime, boating down the Thames, taking in the Tower of London and Shakespeare's playhouse along with other notable attractions. It's a memorable day in the making (though you did miss Queen Mary and General Montgomery in church) and then some guy, filled with despair and wanting to end it all, jumps off a bridge and ruins everything. The guy's got a lot of nerve.

That, of course, wasn't Clara's reaction to the jumper. She was an empathetic person, and her empathy for the jumper brought feelings of depression, not anger. Still, it serves as a reminder that unbearable despair can be encountered at any time or place, even on a trip of a lifetime. I can only speculate that the jumper might have been better served by going to Orators' Row in Hyde Park and venting his misery there.

I'm guessing that Clara's Orators' Row is the same locus of loquaciousness that today is known as Speakers' Corner, as it was called when I visited Hyde Park nineteen years after Clara did. Speakers' Corner is a must for any visit to London, and for my money a better bet than the changing of the guard at Buckingham Palace. The changing of the guard is all about precision, nothing varies. At Speakers' Corner, on the other hand, variation is the rule of the day; one never knows what to expect. You might encounter a fellow on a stepladder extolling the virtues of single world government, while across the way another might be advocating anarchy. The end of the world is popular at Speakers' Corner, whether through nuclear annihilation or the Rapture. Any political philosophy or religion is fair game, as are dire warnings about corporate connivance and looming environmental disasters.

Over the years Speakers' Corner has seen its share of notables, including Karl Marx, Vladimir Lenin, and George Orwell, but its true magic rises from its commonness. You don't have to be famous. If you've got a bee in your bonnet and the gumption to stand up and talk about it, then you'll get a hearing at Speakers' Corner. You may find that no one agrees with you; you might get heckled, but you'll have your say.

Years ago common folk didn't read. Kings and priests did the peoples' learning for them, but then the printing press came along and changed everything. Part of that change meant freedom. Freedom is rarely bestowed; it is usually won through long and difficult struggle. The kings and priests, or whoever holds power at the moment, don't give it up readily. As an intelligent, college-educated woman, Clara surely understood this, for she was denied the right to vote for a full seven years after her graduation, while a man who could barely read was deemed worthy of marking a ballot. The Nineteenth Amendment to the U.S. Constitution remedied that, a much wiser amendment than the one that preceded it and gave us Prohibition.

Places like Speakers' Corner are essential to the continued growth of freedom. In America we're so serious about our First Amendment right to free speech that at times it's hard to sort through the din and all the splashing in the shallow end of the pool. And that's what is special about Speakers' Corner. It's not just a place to make noise. It's a place with reverence for oratory and ideas, and with that reverence comes grace.

Clara was a woman of graceful speech. She was well educated, well read, and curious, all of which worked to make her well-spoken. Then over the last six or so years of her life, she suffered a series of strokes, each of them taking a greater toll on her ability to speak. She would struggle to find words, then struggle to utter them. At other times words would pop out of her mouth that she'd had no intention of saying, often to comical effect. Whenever that happened she would look briefly surprised, then invariably have a laugh at her own expense before returning to the ever-more difficult task of speaking her mind. You might say that she spoke with grace right up to the end.

CHAPTER 6

QUERENCIA

Friday, May 28th

Dearest Clara,

Just checked the itinerary and since I will probably be at the lake the next two or three days thought I had better drop you a note so as to be sure you receive it in Belgium. Not much to write about as I guess the last letter I wrote was Wednesday. Am still missing you very much even tho I have been kept busy every minute. Drove out to the lake this morning and took the windows out and also the double bunks. Thought they might as well go too since I was taking the truck. Warners are to come out early tomorrow morning to put in the windows so I am going out as soon as I get this letter written so as to be sure to be there when they arrive. Have myself a steak and a few potatoes, onions, bacon and eggs, so I should have plenty to eat. Do wish you were here to go with me as it really is kind of lonesome out there alone. Gunder and Fat Morse are supposed to take his outhouse out tonight so they may be there awhile. Said that it needed some repairs so he is fixing it up before taking it out. Guess he and some other Swedes were out there last nite for a picnic. S'pose there will be another mob around the lots on Sunday.

Jacobson's usual company is coming out and guess they expect to picnic on Sunday. Guess they weren't too pleased to have them come as their house is still torn up. Charles and Fritzie said they would be out Sunday and I s'pose they will bring company. They aren't going to Austin until Monday and they intend to stay overnite. Guess they did quite a bit of shopping in the city the other day. Studio couch, a couple of chairs, a dinette set, lamp, and I don't know what else.

We were over and looked the house over last nite, and it doesn't look too bad. Guess they expect to get Warners the first of the week to do their remodeling. Charles, the kids and I set out the tomato plants last nite. The kids were a great help. Has been cool today so should be good for the plants. Came down to the office afterward and worked till about ten on figures. Got home and Mary Russell was there. Went right to bed, but didn't sleep too good. Every morning when I wake up I look over to your bed and for a minute can't figure why it is empty. Will be so glad when you are there again.

Got your letter written on the boat and it sounded like it must be nice. You didn't mention what kind of food you had, tho I imagine the English feed pretty good. Has been trying to rain today, but nothing so far. Surely need it. Am going to start the sprinklers the first of next week if we don't get rain. The yard really looks kind of tough.

Had a letter from Ella today. Said they were planning on coming north in July and if they had a family reunion they would like to get a cottage for the first two weeks in July, and since you were gone was wondering if they couldn't get ours for that time, or if not could I suggest someplace they could get. She said there would be 4 children besides Warren, Sally and herself, so of course they couldn't expect to get in anyone's home. Will write and tell her that you will be here the first two weeks in July and that you will probably want to spend all the time out there you can. Am sure I don't want all of them around here for two weeks.

Guess I had better get this mailed as it is nearly six. I am missing you and thinking of you all the time, Clara, and will be so glad when you get back. I know you are enjoying it, however, and am glad that you have the chance to see the things you are seeing. Have a great time and take care of yourself.

All my love, Ben

We have a pattern emerging in Ben and Clara's letters. Clara writes of her travels, of crossing oceans and visiting great cities like London and Paris. She's on a grand adventure and she describes it from each stop along the way. Ben, on the other hand, writes with an eye on the itinerary and a desire that Clara receive a letter from him at each stop. He writes because timing demands it, not because he has that much to say. Where Clara's letters are adventurous, Ben's are newsy, as in his latest effort with its update on the serial dramas of Gunder Hoaglund's outhouse and the new windows for the cottage.

Ben delivered bunk beds to the lake along with the windows. Those were the same storied bunk beds from which my cousins and I would later peer over the partition and down into the kitchen when Clara was making pancakes, but they came to the lake in 1948 already having a history. They were, in fact, POW beds.

During World War II a number of German prisoners of war ended up in the Olivia area. This was not a vindictive act, intended to inflict the misery of Minnesota winter on the enemy. Rather, the reasoning was pure economics. With all the local farm boys off fighting the war, there was a serious shortage of manpower to do fieldwork, and since the Huns had to be put somewhere, they were put where they could be useful. All summer long they toiled in the fields; then near summer's end when the Olivia Canning Company started its canning season they were put to work there. To accommodate the prisoners, a POW camp was built just west of the canning company. It consisted of six cabins, each measuring about 12' x 20', and a camp administration building of the same size. Each morning the camp guards would march the prisoners down to the plant, where they would put in a twelve- to fifteen-hour day, after which they'd be marched back again. Gunder Hoaglund, magnanimous Swede that he was, allowed that the Germans were a pretty good crew, if for no other reason than their absenteeism was nonexistent. With the war's end, the POWs went home and the government turned the camp over to the canning company to be used as migrant labor housing, complete with bunk beds. The camp administration building was moved next to the boiler room and became the previously mentioned cook shack.

Ben also reported on my parents' successful trip to the Cities to buy furniture for the house we were about to move into. His listing of their purchases made no mention of beds for kids. That's because Judy and I got to sleep in POW bunk beds at home as well as at the lake. We didn't really mind. The beds were available and reasonably comfortable and most likely constructed in accordance with regulations established by the Geneva Convention. Can you say that about your bed?

Once again it's worth taking a moment to read between Ben's lines for deeper meaning. When he wrote of planting tomatoes and said, "The kids were a great help," we can be fairly certain those words were adrip with sarcasm. I don't take that personally. After all, I was two and Judy was four. What did he expect—German POWs?

Ben's feelings about the lake are revealed in two other comments. First, there was his expectation that another mob would come around that Sunday, with his use of the word "mob" implying a crowd not

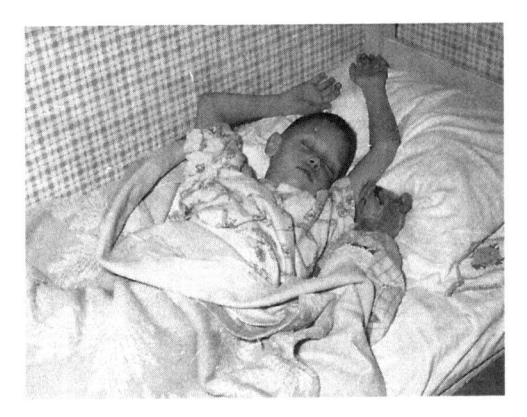

THE AUTHOR IN HIS POW BUNK BED. THIS PHOTO IS EVIDENCE OF HIS FATHER'S PAPARAZZI TENDENCIES. NO ONE WAS SAFE FROM HIS LENS AT ANY TIME, UNDER ANY CIRCUMSTANCE. THE TEDDY BEAR WAS NAMED MUSTARD AND, LIKE THE BED, WAS ACQUIRED SECONDHAND.

happily received. Second, after relating the request from some person named Ella to use the cottage in July, Ben wrote, "Am sure I don't want all of them around here for two weeks." These comments make him sound a bit like an antisocial, grumpy old man. In truth, he could be on the crusty side at times, but I prefer to think of his remarks as a yearning for his *querencia*.

Querencia is a Spanish word that I first came upon in the prologue of William F. Buckley's *Racing Through Paradise*, a book about sailing across the Pacific. As Buckley noted, the word doesn't have an English equivalent. Querencia describes a particular area in a bull ring where the bull imagines itself to be safe and secure. For a matador hoping to reach old age it's important to understand where the bull's querencia is, for he must not stand between it and the bull, lest the bull deviate toward his querencia rather than charging the cape. And so, Buckley notes, querencia becomes an apt metaphor for that special place in life's arena where one feels safe and happy, a place where one longs to be.

The lake was Ben's querencia. His letters reveal his longing to be there, and also his longing to have Clara there with him. She was part of his querencia—she added to it—but it's clear that, for Ben, mobs next door and uninvited guests added nothing. He was set in his ways, I suppose; he wanted the lake on his terms, terms that specified not only how many people should be around, but also what sort of activities might be acceptable. He owned a fourteen-foot aluminum fishing boat with a 7½-hp motor. It was all he needed; he couldn't understand how anyone could need more, so when larger, faster boats began appearing—many with water skiers in tow—he took it as a noisy intrusion into his querencia.

In our early teens Judy and I both learned to ski behind other people's boats, and we were soon badgering Dad for a boat of our own. He relented and bought a pretty fiberglass job with a 50-hp motor. We were ecstatic, but Ben could only shake his head.

One Sunday afternoon Judy and I were skiing—I'd drive the boat while she skied; then she would do the same for me. Watching from shaded chairs on shore were Ben and Clara, my parents and their friends, Dick and Polly. After a while Polly decided she wanted to give water skiing a try, so following our usual division of labor when initiating a novice skier, I was in the boat and Judy was in the water, offering encouragement and instruction. All was set. Polly yelled, "Hit it!" I shoved the throttle forward, and to everyone's surprise she popped right up the very first time. Well, almost up. Her skis came out of the water, but for some reason she didn't straighten her legs, leaving her to skim along, hunched down on her haunches, her bottom dragging in the water. She skied on like that for a goodly distance before finally falling, at which time Ben chuckled and remarked wryly, "First time I ever saw a hundred-yard douche." Spoken like a man in his querencia.

One final observation from Ben's letter: Seems as if Ben's lawn was beginning to resemble the withered summer vegetation on Mars as described by that noted Soviet astro-botanist Gavril Tikhov.

CHAPTER 7

METHODISTS AT THE FOLIES BERGERE

Palace Hotel, Brussels, June 2

My own dearest Ben,

This was a red letter day for me. I got your letter this morning before I left Paris and there was one waiting for me here when I arrived. It was so good to hear from you and you didn't seem so far away when I could know what you were doing just last Friday. It sure gave me a lift to get the letters—the first I've heard from you. I pestered the mail desk in London, asked for a letter every time I went past. It likely came in on the mail just after we left, but I left a forwarding address to Oslo, so hoped to have it there. I have a suspicion that my letter arrived in Paris before this morning, and that the man at the desk didn't understand what I was asking for. Anyway, I was happy to get it—also got Shirley's letter. I have wished so many times that I were at the lake with you. I imagine you had a big time over the weekend, doing your own cooking, but with a lot of company. Quite a while since I've had steak, of course I've had lobster a number of times. We did have good meals on the ship, and I enjoyed most of them. I thought it best to eat lightly, and at times I didn't have too much of an appetite, so I guess that's why I didn't speak much about the meals. I think had I been able to get outside more I would have felt better. It was cloudy and cold the whole crossing, we saw very little of the sun and that weather seems to be holding out. Too bad you don't have some of the rain we are having here.

Yesterday in Paris started out lovely and sunny and warmer than England. We got up rather early to be ready for our first tour at 9:30. We went in a big bus thru what they call modern France—around Napoleon's time. The guide had to tell everything in Portuguese, French, English and Dutch, as he had all those nationalities in the bus. We hit the high spots, among them the Arc de Triomphe and the Unknown Soldier's grave, Eiffel Tower and the Church of Les Invalides where Napoleon is buried. At noon we were just starting out for the restaurant the agency recommended when it started to rain, and we'd left our raincoats at the hotel. It really poured down for a while, so we stood in a doorway till it was over, and wasted precious time. Leo had left his raincoat in the train the day before and never expected to see it again. At the depot this morning he enquired at the lost & found and there it was. After the rain stopped we had quite a time to find our restaurant, and then had to eat hurriedly to get back for our afternoon tour. We had planned to do some shopping in the noon hour and were disappointed not to have the time. In the afternoon we visited the old and historic section of the city. Drove along the Left Bank and the oldest section which is on the island. We visited a couple beautiful churches—Notre Dame Cathedral and Sacre Coeur, which was situated high above the city and gave a wonderful view of it all. We visited the Louvre, but of course had no time to go inside. Two thing I am disappointed not to see in Paris were the Louvre and the

Gardens at Versailles, and we could have done that if we'd had another day, and that would have been so much better than 3 days here in Brussels. S'pose we will be kept busy here tho, and am glad to have the chance to relax and rest a bit, as we have been pretty strenuous since we landed. There was no time to shop after our tour so we went back to our hotel to clean up and have dinner. The hotel was small but very clean, and very nice. We had a suite, and I slept in the parlor and had my own bath. Beds so far have been good, and I sleep well. The hotel here is quite a large hotel and very nice. I have a big double bed full of pillows, so should be comfy. In England we had no napkins and our bath towels were huge—about two yards square, enough to wrap up entirely in. In France we had soft paper napkins, no water is served at the table. Yesterday Leo and I had a bottle of wine for lunch, as we were so thirsty. Leo said it went to his head and he felt queer all afternoon.

In the evening Bertha and Leo wanted to see a show, so I talked them into the Folies Bergere. I told them what to expect, and they were duly shocked. Most of it was very beautiful—costumes, music and stage settings. Parts I didn't care for, but I'm glad we went and I really enjoyed it. We got home at midnight and up this morning at 7 o'clock, so as to have breakfast and be ready to go to the depot by 8:30, tho our train didn't leave till 9:30. Woke up to another rainy day—a steady drizzle—and it rained all the way here so we couldn't see too much of the country. There were 5 others in our compartment and most could speak English, so we visited more or less. We got here at 1:30 and were met by our agent who brought us to the hotel. We went down to eat as soon as we could, as we hadn't eaten on the train. Had very good food here at the hotel. They say everything costs more here—we get 45 francs for a dollar, while in France we got 300. Leo and I had quite a time not to get too many as we didn't want any French francs left over. We didn't spend much in Paris. I cashed my first check here today and still have about $70, so should make out. S'pose when I get to shopping my money will go.

You seem to be keeping plenty busy. S'pose by now the windows are all on, I'm so anxious to see them. Am anxious to see the furniture the kids bought. Am lonesome for you all, and I keep thinking of you, Ben, and how much more fun it would be to have you with me. I really think you'd like Paris. It is quite fascinating; it has something hard to define. Take it easy my dearest, and take good care of my you. I love you all so much and am lonely for you. Give my love to Charles, Fritzie, Judy and Chuckie.

All my love, Clara

That the wine went to Leo's head and made him feel "queer" all afternoon serves as yet another reminder that words, like the previously mentioned "gaily clad men," can take on new meaning over time. We can be fairly certain that the wine did not cause Leo to have amorous feelings for his table waiter.

Clara's letters mention their agent from time to time, a ubiquitous fellow who sometimes meets their trains, arranges tours, recommends restaurants, and generally facilitates their travels. Having an agent seems sensible for travelers of Clara's age, especially ones making their first trip abroad. Facilitated travel taken to the extreme was illustrated in the 1969 movie *If It's Tuesday, This Must Be Belgium*. The movie portrays folks traveling Europe on a bus who are so insulated from the countries and cultures they pass through that the only way to know where they are is to consult their schedule. That's no way to travel if your goal is to actually experience different cultures. I get the sense from Clara's letters that their degree of facilitated travel was about right. They got some help along the way, but not so much as to keep them from rubbing foreign shoulders. Still, as I read her letters I couldn't help but contrast her travels with my own first trip to Europe.

It was 1967, the summer between my junior and senior years in college. My college had a program called SWAP, which stood for Student Work Abroad Project. It wasn't about studying abroad. Rather it was simply about packing students off to Europe for three months in the summer to be broadened by traveling through and living in different cultures. To make it affordable the college found each of us a job for two months, leaving the third month free for travel. I guess you could say that the college functioned as our agent, but only to a limited extent. Basically, they arranged a cheap, round-trip charter flight from Minneapolis to Paris, instructed us to show up for our jobs on time and not embarrass the college, then be back in Paris at the end of August in time for the flight home. Beyond that we were on our own.

My job was in a hotel in the Scottish Highlands where I worked as a waiter in the dining room, a job made more difficult by the fact that we did French service. With French service you don't get to simply plunk down a plateful of food in front of each customer. That would be the easy way, the American way, but the French like to complicate things. French service requires that an *empty* plate be placed in front of each person. Then I would come along in my starched white jacket, a towel over my arm, and serve each portion—meat, potatoes, vegetable, whatever—onto their plates from platters I held in one hand while wielding a fork and spoon in my other hand. Some foods were easier to serve than others. I scattered a lot of peas around the dining room that summer. I had never been a fan of Brussels sprouts, nor am I now, but I did come to appreciate them for their ease of handling.

For my month of traveling I teamed up with my friend Jim. We traveled light, each with a single small bag, and we covered a lot of ground. At times when the scenery was particularly compelling—Switzerland and Austria—we hitchhiked. Other times we rode the trains. Our usual strategy was to take overnight trains, thereby saving the cost of a hotel room. One night that strategy took a rather dramatic twist.

The Cold War was in full force in 1967. Berlin was still a divided city and Germany was still a divided country. Against that backdrop, Jim and I boarded a train in West Berlin one night with the expectation that it would deliver us to Amsterdam the following morning. We settled into a second-class compartment (traveling cheap), ready for an uneventful night on the train, but it wasn't to be. Half an hour out of Berlin we made our first stop, where uniformed East German guards boarded the train and proceeded to go from compartment to compartment, demanding to see passports. When an officious-looking fellow demanded ours, we handed them over, thinking it was nothing more than a bureaucratic nuisance, but upon inspecting our passports the guard began barking at us in German. Now the German that Jim and I spoke was good for buying beer and bratwurst, and maybe renting a hotel room, but not a lot more, so we had no idea what the fellow was going on about. Still, we held to the hope that it was just some perfunctory Cold War swagger, that he would have his say and then we would be on our way, but to our dismay he started down the corridor with our passports in hand, signaling for us to follow. We had no choice but to do so; it wasn't wise to get separated from your passport in the middle of East Germany. We followed him off the train and onto the platform where our Tower-of-Babel discussion resumed. We also became aware of other guards on the platform, some armed with submachine guns and accompanied by large dogs. Things were not looking good, and then things got decidedly worse as our train began pulling out of the station, leaving us behind in the East German night.

Eventually the situation got sorted out. An English-speaking guard magically appeared and explained that we had a visa problem. Seems that during another Tower-of-Babel discussion a few days earlier while transiting into Berlin we had mistakenly acquired what amounted to one-way visas. We could get into town, but not out. Now we filled out forms, paid tribute in the form of cigarettes to one of the guards, then boarded a local train that would take us back to West Berlin. The next day we bought the proper visas and boarded the train again that night, arriving the following morning in Amsterdam, only a day later than we had planned. Yes, it all worked out, but before it did there had been that awful sinking feeling as our train departed into the night, leaving us on that East German platform. At that moment I could have used an agent . . . or my mother.

Clara regretted not having time for the Louvre or the Gardens at Versailles, but to her credit she did talk Bertha and Leo into the Folies Bergere. The Folies Bergere is a long-established icon of Paris nightlife, known for its music, dancing, extravagant sets and costumes, and yes, a good deal of nudity. It was the nudity, no doubt, that duly shocked Bertha and Leo, but Clara thought most of it very beautiful and she really enjoyed the performance. She was intellectually curious, particularly so when it came to the arts and culture. There were parts of the show she didn't care for, but she wasn't one to drape Venus de Milo. She knew good art and beauty when she saw it, and ironically it was Clara, my grandmother, who became my most reliable boyhood source for nude photography.

At the time I was perhaps twelve, and to be sure, twelve-year-old boys growing up in Olivia in the 1950s didn't have many sources for nude photography. *Playboy* was sold at the drugstore, but the pharmacist conspired with the town mothers to deny the magazine to anyone under the age of eighteen—the very demographic that needed it most! One time I did manage to acquire a true treasure. It was a photography magazine that usually dealt with cameras and lenses and the nuts and bolts of photography, but once a year, in the manner of *Sports Illustrated's* swimsuit edition, it devoted an entire issue to baring female delights. It had somehow come into the possession of a kid I knew and he sold it to me for the princely sum of seventy-five cents. Informed by my twelve-year-old-boy sensibilities, I knew that such a treasure had to be kept hidden, so I secreted it away in the springs beneath my mattress. Who would ever look there? The problem with twelve-year-old-boy sensibilities is that they don't take into account things like spring housecleaning, so one day I came home from school to find my treasure sitting on the kitchen counter. Ah, paradise lost, and to make matters worse, I had to endure my mother's lecture about the sort periodicals a "good boy" does and does not read. Rest assured there was nary a nipple to be found on the approved list.

So it was that Clara, my culturally curious grandmother, became my chief source for photos of nature's best artistic effort: female breasts. Unlike those fibbing *Playboy* subscribers, Clara actually did take *National Geographic* for the articles. She wanted to know about the world she lived in, and occasionally the magazine featured tribes from the jungles of Africa or far up the Amazon, tribes whose womenfolk often went around bare-breasted. Clara wanted me to know about the world I lived in too, so she happily shared her *National Geographics* with me, and I happily perused them, though admittedly I spent more time on the photos than the articles. Not exactly a walk on the wild side, you say, but a twelve-year-old boy in the 1950s took what he could get.

I hasten to add here that I am no more taken with female breasts than the average guy, lest you think me obsessive on the subject. True, each of the three novels I have published to date make mention of breasts from time to time, but that only puts me in a large company of writers, male and female. I could further argue that breasts are hard to ignore. They're right there in front for all to see, and women do tend to choose clothing that confirms, rather than denies, their existence. I could offer those defenses, but instead I will simply note that Carlos Eire chose to begin his wonderful book *Waiting for Snow in Havana* with this quote from a Charles Simic poem: "I spit on fools who fail to include breasts in their metaphysics, Stargazers who have not enumerated them among the moons of the earth." *Waiting for Snow in Havana* won the National Book Award, so Carlos Eire is no boob. And that's all I'm going to say about breasts . . . for now, anyway.

CHAPTER 8

GOLF

Tuesday Eve. June 1ˢᵗ

Dearest Clara,

Guess the last time I wrote you was on Friday just before going to the lake. I went out there that nite and the next morning two of the Warners showed up and on Saturday we got the windows in and some shelves in the corner. Tried to get them to build an end table to fit on the end of the davenport but they were anxious to get back to town so couldn't get them to do it. The windows really look nice and I am sure you are going to like them. Guess I must have picked up a flu bug of some kind as I didn't feel too good Friday nite. On Saturday I felt worse, but felt a little better Sunday. Yesterday I slept a good share of the afternoon, but began to feel pretty punk in the evening. Was going to stay out there last nite but it got so lonesome and I didn't think it was too good to be out there alone if I was going to be sick, so decided to come to town. Didn't feel very good this morning and haven't had much pep all day, but feel better tonite. Didn't have much commotion at the lake. No one out there Saturday except the Warners, Gunder and me. On Sunday Hoaglunds were out and also Jacobsons and their company. Charles and Fritzie were out in the afternoon and stayed for supper. Yesterday Gunder and family were the only ones who showed up. Schulers were out and I spent part of Friday evening with them. They came over Saturday nite for about an hour. Had dinner with them yesterday noon. Guess they will be out again next weekend. Gets awful lonesome out there alone and I certainly miss having you there. Really don't know what to do with myself. Cleaned up the shack Sunday morning but it has been so dry that there is no lawn to mow so didn't have too much work. Guess I won't get out there for a while now as Cohn will arrive Thurs. to audit the books and I will have to get ready for him and then stick around while he is here. The Heinz crowd were all out there yesterday with Barkows and the Ernie Lowes. They look about the same, tho I think he has taken on some weight. Have been busy on the books all day today. Had to serve at the golf club tonite and just came from there. I was chairman with Gunder and Quent Brandt. Gunder did most of the work however, which was quite a change for me. Had meatballs and scalloped potatoes, pickles, bread and butter and glazed donuts. Were only about 15 out. There doesn't seem to be too much interest as only a few were playing golf. Charles and Fritzie went to Austin early this morning and came back tonite. Was just home and Charles said they had a rather rugged day with the kids. Fritzie had gone over to Eric's so didn't see her. Came out 20 cents ahead on the feed tonite so didn't go behind anyway. Also had a few potatoes and donuts to take home. Went fishing a couple of times over the weekend but guess the fish have deserted our lake as I didn't get any. Just as well as I didn't have to clean them. Am still driving the car around so should have it broken in by the time you get back. It's getting awfully dirty however, but as long as it stays so dusty can't see much point in washing it. Like it better right along.

Everyone asks about you but haven't been able to give them much information so far. Hope I will be getting a letter most any time now as you should have landed Saturday. Hope my letter was waiting there for you. Still is terribly dry here. The lawn is burning up and I'll have to get the sprinklers out if we are to have any lawn. Guess we didn't have a bit of rain during May, which is unusual. The garden isn't doing much either and am afraid our first radishes have gone bye. Should be thru planting corn by the end of the week. Have left most of that to Charles. Had hoped to have a letter from Shirley today to send along with this but didn't get anything.

Had figured on doing some work at the office tonite but feel rather tired so think I will go home and go to bed. Am still missing you terribly and will be so glad when you get back. Still a month to wait and that is going to be a long one. Hope you are getting lots of sightseeing now. Will be so glad to hear from you, as it is a long time since your last letter. Have a good time and think of all of us back home. We all miss you.

All my love, Ben

Ben's letter skips around more than usual. Picture him sitting in his office on a Tuesday night, reflecting on the long Memorial Day weekend. He seems to have a lot on his mind and his thoughts pinball back and forth. He begins with news from the lake and an update on the new windows—no surprise there. Next comes a day-by-day narrative of his brush with some sort of flu bug; then it's back to the lake for more news, followed by a sentence or two on office matters and the pending audit. Once more to the lake then before moving on to the golf club. He pauses here to write of my parents' trip to Austin, MN (a Memorial Day visit to the graves of my mother's parents), then back to the golf club for a leftovers report. And finally, to the lake yet again for fishing news. We should excuse Ben's ramblings. It's been a long day, he's been sick, and there's an audit pending; plus, he misses his wife terribly. Then, too, he has just come from the golf club where he might well have chipped a couple in at the nineteenth hole.

This isn't Ben's first mention of the golf club. Sports were important to him. In college he played second base on the Hamline baseball team; later golf competed with the lake for his leisure time. Indeed, Ben was a charter member of the Olivia Golf Club as well as one of its original organizers. My family's ties to the club grew stronger still with my dad, who was bitten early by the golf bug and went on to become a three-time club champion.

As long as anyone can remember, Tuesday has been designated as the club's men's night, a chauvinistic claiming of the course for guys only: an afternoon of golf, followed by camaraderie at the nineteenth hole and supper, then perhaps a card game or two and more visits to the nineteenth hole. Women make their claim on Thursday, though instead of women's night, they have ladies' day: golf sandwiched around a noon luncheon. I've never fully understood why the men have a night and the women have a day. It's usually shrugged off as a guy/gal thing: just what everyone prefers. Could be, but I suspect that it might have something to do with who is expected to be home fixing supper on Thursday night.

The supper menu Ben described—meatballs, scalloped potatoes, pickles, bread and butter, and glazed donuts—sounds like a guy concoction. It seems in 1948 they had a revolving committee system with different members being responsible for the Tuesday night feed each week. Ben came out twenty cents and a few potatoes and donuts ahead. Implied in that was the apparent risk that the responsible members might actually lose money. By the time I joined the club they had a better system: buy a steak from the club and grill it yourself, thereby limiting the chance of losing money to your misfortunes on the golf course or at the card table.

In 1955 Ben and Clara's ties to the golf club grew even closer, as the house they built that year—the house where I now live—abuts the course. Prior to that, the course had been bordered to the east and south by farm fields. Seeing an investment opportunity, Ben and two other local businessmen developed a 33-lot subdivision on the golf course's east side, with each of the three partners claiming a prime lot next to the course. The subdivision is situated on a slight rise of land, prompting it to be rather pretentiously named the Hillcrest Addition. That it's called a hill at all is testament to Olivians being confirmed flatlanders. When visitors from more vertical parts of the world are introduced to the neighborhood, they invariably look quizzically about and ask, "Hill?" I've long suspected that the Hillcrest name was someone's idea of a joke, and supporting that theory is the fact that Hill*crest* Avenue runs along the *bottom* of the hill.

In local speak, Hillcrest was soon shortened to "The Hill," then expanded again through a process of small-minded envy to "Snob Hill." This was most likely a play on San Francisco's Nob Hill, which is a real hill with real estate values worthy of the word snob. Connecting Olivia to such a lofty place is quite a reach, and to be sure, no one ever wrote a song about leaving their heart in Olivia. I suppose the snob part arose from the fact that the homes built there were the newer ones in town. Today it's a neighborhood of unpretentious 1950s and 1960s ranches and ramblers, a number of them with single-car garages. Hardly the stuff of snobbery, yet to some it's still Snob Hill. I guess envy dies hard.

So now I have come to live on the golf course. I played the game on and off for over thirty years, though never with my father's prowess, and eventually it got to the point where the only reason I played was because other people thought I should. This struck me as an odd way for an adult to conduct his life, so I gave it up, but not playing the game doesn't in any way diminish my enjoyment of living on the course. It's like hunting, something else I no longer do, but I still love seeing the ducks and geese pass through the lake each spring and fall.

Having a golf club next door isn't different from having any other kind of neighbor in that good neighborliness is a two-way street—in addition to appreciating our neighbor's good points, we must also tolerate their foibles. The golf club's chief foible is the penchant its members have for hitting golf balls into my yard and occasionally thwacking them off my walls. In Ben's day the eighth fairway ran past the house, but the course was reconfigured and we are now adjacent to the practice range. A practice range is by definition a place one goes when they are in need of practice, and if the errant shots landing in our yard are any indication, a number of these folks truly need the practice. For my part, I'm happy to toss the balls back whenever I mow the lawn. In return the club tends and waters its fairways while maintaining a pleasing variety of trees, all of which provide a lush, green summertime panorama. In winter it's almost lovelier, with bare trees casting long afternoon shadows across a dazzling white snowfield—and no golf balls bouncing into my yard.

CHAPTER 9

ROCK-RIBBED REPUBLICANS

Monday morning, Copenhagen

My Dearest Ben,

We arrived here late last evening so I went right to bed, have just had breakfast so will write you right away. Your letter was waiting for me when I arrived and I was so happy to get it. You seem so far away and the time has been so long since I saw you, and when I think how much longer it is going to be, I wish I were home this very minute. I certainly am never again going to leave you for so long a time. Nothing is worth it. I am so lonely for you and miss you so all the time.

Was sorry to hear you had been sick and hope you are fine again. I kept wishing I could be out to the lake with you. Am so anxious to see the new windows and shelves. It's hard to imagine everything so dry, as yesterday is the first day on our trip that it hasn't rained. It was raining Sat. eve when we left Brussels but cleared up about noon yesterday. We didn't dare stir out without our raincoats—most of the rain was in showers, tho, so we could get places between showers.

We had quite a leisurely time in Brussels. It is quite a bustling city—seemed to be plenty of money—everywhere we saw

American cars: Buicks, Cadillacs, Studebakers, Chevys, etc.—all new. When we had nothing else to do it was interesting just to watch out of our hotel window, which overlooked a square where all sorts of folks were crossing all the time. There were women in wooden shoes who had flower stalls, which were colorful. Leo is busy taking pictures, but never has his camera at the right time. He has a $24 light meter, but he never uses it, so am wondering if he will get any pictures that are good.

Thurs. morning in Brussels we took a tour over the city—most interesting to me was the old Town Hall, built in the oldest part of the city. It was built in 1,400—plenty old—and in lovely Gothic architecture. This square is also surrounded by the old guild houses and the King's house—all old and the square filled with flower stalls. We visited an art gallery—all the paintings done by one man, and very interesting. We saw the king's palace, visited some churches, and of course stopped at a lace factory. We were supposed to buy some lace-a-la-Havana but we didn't. In the afternoon, tho, our agent took us to a lace shop where we bought a few pieces. Then we walked back to our hotel quite a distance, but we took it leisurely and enjoyed it. That evening we wandered down a street and then ate at the same place we had been the night before.

Friday it rained all morning, so spent most of the time in our rooms—we had connecting rooms, which was nice. In the afternoon we went on a tour out to the site of the Battle of Waterloo. A lovely drive out, tho part of the way over cobblestone pavement which shook me most to pieces. We drove out the highway which leads to Germany and by which the Germans entered Brussels. Part of the way was thru the Forest of Soigne—beautiful tall trees. The Germans used these woods as an ammunition dump, and some shells are still buried there. In the center of the battlefield is a huge mound of dirt, all of which was brought in baskets on the backs of women as a memorial to the dead. They worked for 2 years and it covers most of the dead men and horses who fell there. We visited a panorama of the battle which was very interesting. That evening I went to bed early, as I felt like I had the flu coming on—head and back ache—had a good rest and felt better, but stayed in all morning. Leo and Bertha took a streetcar ride. In the afternoon we went over to the old part of town and I got some wooden shoes for Jeffie.

We left town at 6:00. The depot was near the hotel so we walked over. I had a cup of chocolate before I left, so didn't eat on the train, as I didn't feel too good. We had connecting compartments, and I went to bed early. We stopped a long while at Aachen on the border and there seemed to be some commotion. Bertha told me I'd better get up as we might have to get off. It seems we were supposed to get a permit to go across Germany and we had none—our agency had slipped up somewhere. It was in the British occupied area and the inspector finally said we could go as they had passed us in England. Quite a relief. We rode thru Germany all night and till noon, and saw plenty of destruction, especially along R.R. tracks in cities. We got off just before the Danish border and went thru both German and Danish customs—no searching of baggage except looking thru one on the train. In Denmark they ran the train onto a ferry. We went up on deck and had a lovely ride—about 1½ hours. We had lunch on the ferry, then back on the train and to Copenhagen. The sun is still shining—a most welcome sight. We are going out to see the city now. I miss you so.

All my love, Clara

P.S. Have the plants I put out by the side of the house dried up?

Clara and Bertha and Leo fared better than I when they tried crossing Germany without the required documents, but then they got to deal with the British, whereas I tangled with the East Germans. It's nice to have allies.

Clara does more than simply report the passing attractions. Her letters detail the background and history of the places they visit, as with the German use of the Forest of Soigne as a munitions dump or the mound-of-dirt memorial at the site of the Battle of Waterloo. This inclination comes as no surprise, as Clara was a storyteller, and she always told her stories with a purpose in mind.

From time to time my sister, Judy, and I would be left in Clara's care while our parents attended to one thing or another, and that was never a problem. We loved going to Clara's, as much for her utter disregard for our dental health—she exercised a grandmother's prerogative to feed a sweet tooth—as for any other reason. There will be more on Clara's cornucopia of sweets in a coming chapter, but for now suffice it to say that sugar highs were inevitable at her house. To her credit, though, she didn't stoke our blood sugar without taking responsibility, and her usual antidote was to sit us down and read us a story.

Clara's bookshelves held numerous volumes of children's stories from which she could choose. Those stories were best described as classics with a European bias, tales of princes and princesses and gallant knights, people of rank meeting great challenges with a sense of noblesse oblige. In meeting the tests, these true hearts would invariably display the sort of virtues a grandmother seeks to instill in those she reads to, virtues that go beyond mere gallantry. In short, grandmother virtues. Clara's stories touted character and loyalty and thoughtfulness and caring and honesty and on and on. She had lots of books, and they covered almost any virtue you could think of with one glaring exception. As already noted, her stories had a European bias, so they failed to convey that one concept Americans are always going on about to the irritation of everyone else in the world: American exceptionalism. Clara did more than merely read stories; she was also known to spin a pretty good yarn, and that's just what she did to close the American exceptionalism gap in her choice of children's literature. What's more, she often customized her stories for the recipient with an eye toward nurturing a needed virtue, and perhaps that's why the ones I most remember were told when I was alone in her company. It's fair to assume she did the same for Judy, only Judy's stories would promote virtue in ways appealing to girls.

The stories Clara made up for me followed a rather predictable template. Start with two boys who were often lucky enough to each own a pony. Sometimes one of the ponies had a white star-like mark on its face, in which case its name would be Star. The boys would pack camping gear and supplies, then saddle their ponies and head into the woods, riding for hours before making camp along a gurgling creek. Being responsible boys, they saw to the ponies first, watering and feeding them before tending to their own creature comforts. The exact spot for pitching the tent was chosen with woodsman-like wisdom, thereby avoiding the calamities associated with mispitched tents. Once the tent was up, a shallow trench was dug around its perimeter to direct water away in the event of heavy rainfall. (In Clara's stories the tents were always trenched in this manner, suggesting that she and Ben had some soggy camping experiences in their early tenting days at the lake before their cottage was built.) Supper usually involved boy-friendly food like hotdogs roasted on sticks over an open fire. A balanced diet was often achieved with blueberries conveniently growing on nearby bushes.

The boys were invariably tested on their camping trips, the test often coming after dark when they were snuggled down in their tent for the night. It might be a fierce thunderstorm, or a visit to the campsite by a raccoon or porcupine or even a bear. Whatever the challenge, the boys always met it with the skill and grace of seasoned frontiersmen, and the next morning the sun would shine and the boys would happily ride out of the woods, all the better for their experience.

The gallant knights of Clara's other stories might slay a dragon or two, but they never rode into the woods just for the sake of doing it, nor did they have the good sense to trench around their tents. That was how Clara depicted American exceptionalism. Americans always go into the woods where challenges are met, not with noblesse oblige, but with the innate wisdom and self-reliance peculiar to the early pioneers. That sense of American exceptionalism shared a common root with another concept held dear by Ben and Clara: rock-ribbed Republicanism.

Rock-ribbed Republicans gather in Olivia to show their support for Dwight Eisenhower. Clara is second row, second from the right. Ben is in the upper right hand corner.

The adjective *rock-ribbed* is no longer in vogue, and that's a shame. Today's occupants of that purportedly big tent are more likely to call themselves true conservatives or social conservatives or Tea Party faithful or some other brand connoting a rigid ideological purity that gets in the way of practical solutions. Not that the rock-ribbed Republicans of Ben and Clara's day were a wishy-washy lot. They stood for integrity and self-reliance, fiscal responsibility and a strong America, but they were also practical. They didn't hate government; they valued good government. They didn't blather on about the size of their tent; they trenched around it. And they liked Ike.

I believe that Clara's stories were seeds carefully planted with the hope that Judy and I would grow to be virtuous people, and that one of those desired virtues was rock-ribbed Republicanism. It didn't take. I'd like to think that at least the rock-ribbed part did, though admittedly rock-ribbed moderate/progressivism is something of an oxymoron. In any event, neither of us is a Republican, but that's the fault of the Republican Party, not Clara.

CHAPTER 10

HALFTIME

We have now reached the midpoint in Ben and Clara's letters, so we will take a one-chapter break from them. Meanwhile, for your halftime entertainment, I offer another letter from my attic, one not written by either Ben or Clara, but one that explains how they came to live in Olivia.

In an earlier chapter we traced the Corneliussen family moves from Norway to Iowa to St. Paul and Hamline University where Clara's life intersected with Ben's. Now it's time for a brief look at Ben's family history.

Of course, Brown is a very common name with many family lines claiming it. From time to time it's been taken as a name of convenience, meaning that a family assumed the name to distance themselves from a horse thief or highwayman in some past generation. A look back through five generations of my family reveals no such scoundrel, only working-class misery in the mills of the industrial revolution in nineteenth-century England.

John Rightson Brown was born to Hugh and Mary Brown in Leeds, England, in 1818. He married Harriett Speight in 1838, then spent the next twenty years toiling in the mills and fathering seven children, all the while yearning to emigrate to America. In 1858 that yearning grew so strong that John and Harriett obtained passage to

New York for the entire family. They ended up on a farm near Augusta, Wisconsin, just east of Eau Claire, and shortly thereafter their eighth child, my great-grandfather Charles (the first of several in the family, it seems) was born.

But John's restless urges weren't yet satisfied. In 1878 the U.S. Government opened prairie land in Minnesota for homestead claims, and John, at age sixty, headed west again along with four of his sons, including Charles, then twenty. John settled in Tyro Township in Yellow Medicine County where he would die nine years later. The sons all settled in the same general area with Charles putting down roots in Hanley Falls. There he farmed and also worked as a stock buyer, traveling the area on horseback, purchasing cattle, and arranging their shipment to St. Paul. He apparently did more than just buy cattle, as a 1904 listing of Hanley Falls businesses included C. A. Brown's butcher shop.

Like his father, John, Charles and his wife, Eunice, had ten children. Ben, born in 1890, was the fourth. Not many lads left the farms of western Minnesota for college in those days, so Ben going to Hamline was a matter of heightened expectations. Perhaps he was inspired by his uncle, Charles's youngest brother, Isaac Newton Brown. If ever a name imposed onerous expectations on a son, Isaac's surely did. Alas, Isaac didn't become a world-famous physicist, but to his credit he did graduate from college and go on to become a schoolteacher.

Whatever the expectations, Ben did go to Hamline where he graduated in the spring of 1913. Turning to the task of finding employment, he made inquiries to fraternity brothers already out in the working world about possible opportunities—that's why one joins a fraternity, after all. In June he received a letter from a fraternity brother who had graduated a year or two before and had joined his family's business. It was addressed simply to Mr. Ben A. Brown, St. Paul, Minn. As a further aid to the postman, "Beta Kappa Fraternity, Hamline University" was added in the lower right-hand corner. The letterhead identified the company as Heins & Byers of Olivia, Minnesota, dealers in hardware, farm machinery, electric supplies, sewing machines, pumps, photographic supplies, vehicles, paints, oils, etc. The inclusion of that "etc." at the end of their long list implied that no matter what you might need, Heins & Byers were the folks to see. Here's the letter:

June 21, 1913

Dear Ben:

Have been away for a few days and did not get your letter until Sunday. We are looking for a man here in the hardware store and I think that what I know from your qualifications you would make good.

Now, I'll tell you, Ben, I do not know what you are looking for or what you expect to find. We want a man who will stay on the job and will learn the business with the intention of giving us the benefit of his learning. We have a need for both a floor man and an outside man who would do canvassing and general outside work. As to the floor man, we will expect whoever we get to learn stock and in time to take care of stock buying as well as keeping shelf goods in shape. As I say, however, at this time of the year we expect to use our men wherever they are needed, most of which is likely to be outside. A man who learns to know machinery and who is of the kind that mixes well with people and gets along with the trade, can be valuable to the firm and draw wages accordingly. Also a man who becomes familiar with shelf hardware and learns to know hardware stock and how to keep it in shape is also able to draw pretty fair salary.

If you thought you would like to try it for the summer at least with the privilege of staying an indefinite time in case you like the work and prove satisfactory, I would be glad to have you consider the position. We could not pay you very much in the way of wages at least until you become somewhat experienced. Having graduated from college you may expect to get something pretty good to start with and possibly you can, but if you like the hardware business I think you will find that we will treat you right and with a few years' experience you will be able to do as well in the hardware business as any.

If you came to us we would want you as soon as possible as this is a busy time of the year. If you think that the proposition looks at all promising to you I would be glad to have you look in the matter fully. If there is anything about the business that you want to know or even you might like to come out and see what things look like, I would be more than glad to have you do so. At least let me hear from you by early mail as we want to get someone at once and I will hold up any other applications until I hear from you.

Yours fraternally,

Warren H. Heins

Ben took Warren up on his offer and moved to Olivia. Initially, his goal was to one day manage a store of his own, but as things turned out his future wasn't in hardware.

In the early years of the twentieth century, the canned food industry was seen as an investment in modern technology with a good profit potential. The movers and shakers of Olivia agreed, and in 1905, just eighteen years after the town was established, they incorporated the Olivia Canning, Preserving and Manufacturing Company, a name that later was mercifully shortened to the Olivia Canning Company. The original shareholders numbered seventy-eight and included area farmers and local businessmen. The Heinses were prominent among those investors; indeed, C. A. Heins was the company's first president.

Ben worked the hardware trade for a few years; then in 1916 he used his Heins connection as an avenue into the canning company's management. He learned the business under its original manager, a fellow named Chapman, then became the manager in 1919. For the next seventy-seven years a Brown would manage the company.

For most of its existence, the company specialized in cream-style corn, adding whole kernel in its last dozen or so years. In its earliest years, however, the product line mirrored the small family farms of the time, producing small amounts of many different things. It was as if the company was willing to can just about any kind of food that found its way to the factory door. Those early products included sauerkraut, tomatoes, peas, pumpkin, rhubarb, string beans, kidney beans, beets, spinach, beet greens, Swiss chard, apples, and of course sweet corn. Canning small amounts of so many different products had to be terribly inefficient, and sound economics soon had the company specializing in sweet corn, but at least one of those early products made a lasting mark on the company's lexicon.

Right up to the company's last days, an area of the plant was called the kraut shed—even though sauerkraut hadn't been canned for over eighty years. The kraut shed got its name from large wooden vats that had once stood in that location. Shredded cabbage and the other necessary ingredients would be loaded into the vats where the mix would then ferment into sauerkraut prior to being canned. That fermentation process could be hastened along with periodic stirring, thus creating the challenge of how best to stir the kraut.

Now, for the span of this one paragraph, allow your thoughts to wander to wine-making in Italy. Imagine comely lasses, their skirts hitched up, stepping barefoot into vats filled with grapes. There's laughter and perhaps music, too, amid much squishing. It's all quite romantic. Allow your thoughts to wander far enough and it can even be erotic, what with all that squishing between bare toes.

Now return your thoughts to the kraut shed where, sadly, nothing was romantic, much less erotic. No comely lasses with hitched-up skirts were called to stir the kraut. That was the job of a male employee who, prior to stepping into a vat, donned a pair of hip boots conveniently hanging on a wall near the vats. He would walk around as best he could—I should think walking in sauerkraut to be difficult—then move on to the next vat.

When I think back on all the government inspections I endured during my years at the Olivia Canning Company, I can at least be thankful that I never had to explain those hip boots to an inspector. And with that, it's back to Ben and Clara's letters.

CHAPTER 11

CURMUDGEONS AND CARPET

Thursday, June 3rd

Dearest Clara,

Had hoped to have a letter today but guess maybe airmail doesn't get over there as fast as some people think. Hope you have been getting all my letters as I have written you with the intention that you would have a letter on your arrival at each place. S'pose tonight you are in Brussels. Seems an awful long ways off and wish you were here instead of so far away, but guess I shouldn't be selfish as I am sure you are enjoying it. Everyone asks what I hear from you but tell them I haven't anything to report so far. Faye and Marjorie just drove by and asked about you and said to tell you hello and to have a good time. Am at the office tonight with the auditor. Cohn didn't show up this year either so have the same fellow here again. I like him just as well or better than Cohn, however, so am satisfied.

Haven't been doing much since I wrote on Tuesday. Yesterday Charles and Emil fertilized our lawn and also at the office and got the sprinklers going and have had them on ever since. Had it in the garden all last evening. Today I have had to run home every hour or so to change them, so between there and the plant I have spent most of the time dragging hose around. Also went home this afternoon and sprayed the weeds in the rose bushes and along the hedge. Have quite a time getting away every time I go home, however, as Chuckie always wants to go for a ride. The kids have both been fine, though they were both pretty irritable today. Guess the heat is too much for them. Has been in the high 80s both yesterday and today, and we aren't used to it. The neighborhood kids were all tearing around in the sprinklers when I was home this p.m. so I told them they had better stay away while the water was on. Still terribly dry. The farmers are beginning to worry about whether there is enough moisture to start the corn. Hope we aren't going to have another year like 1936, when it was so dry and we had all the worms.

Charles has had a couple of the Warners today so he has been there all day, and guess Gunder has been there a good share of the day too. They tore out that partition and then had to put a beam across. They also took out those pillars between the living and dining rooms and built a couple closets. Should be fully nice when they get all thru but am afraid they will find they have quite an expensive house. They had Gordy Schultz over last night and he is going to put in a regular oil heating job for them. Well, it's their money, I guess, so I'm not going to say anything. Haven't driven the car very much lately. Hope to get into Minneapolis sometime next week and have it polished and get the regular 1,000 mile check up on it.

Haven't been out to the lake this week and may not get out there Saturday if the auditor doesn't get thru. He didn't arrive until this noon. I spent the evening here last nite getting some last minute figures so didn't get to bed too early and was up at six this morning. Have felt much better the last couple of days so guess I must have had a bug, all right. Haven't heard any more from Halversons about coming out to the lake and don't know as I shall remind them of it as it is too much work.

Am enclosing another letter from Shirley. Bob certainly has a time with his shirts. Don't think I will attempt to buy him any more. Let him get his own. Charles' birthday will be along in another week. S'pose I should take them out to dinner somewhere since I have been eating pretty regularly on them. Have had practically all my meals there except breakfast and when I have been at the lake.

We all miss you and I still miss you so much. Only half of the time gone too. Hope you have time to miss me a little with all your busy sightseeing. Hope you are keeping a diary. Have a good time. I love you.

All my love, Ben

I've been accused by my own family of being something of a curmudgeon. That may well be true, but if Ben's letter is any indication, I at least came by it honestly. Ben certainly sounded curmudgeonly when he told the neighborhood kids to stay away from his sprinklers when the water was on. What normal, healthy kid can resist a sprinkler on a hot summer day? And if we are to take his words literally, why would a kid run through sprinklers with the water off? Maybe, like his grandchildren, Ben was just irritable that day because of the heat.

If the curmudgeon gene does indeed run in my family, it clearly skipped my father, or if he carried it, it was overwhelmingly dominated by another gene, one he inherited from Clara. To say that Clara was an optimist falls woefully short of the mark. She approached life with what can only be called unrelenting cheerfulness, a trait she passed on to both my dad and his sister, Shirley. When Dad was a boy, Clara gave him a plaque that read:

> Smile and the whole world smiles with you;
>
> Kick, and you kick alone;
>
> For a cheerful grin will let you in,
>
> Where a kicker is never known.

That plaque hung on his wall all his days—he believed it and lived by it—but that's not to cede all the genetic high ground to Clara and relegate Ben to the depths of grumpiness. We curmudgeons need to stick together, after all, and I submit that curmudgeonliness is open to interpretation. My dictionary defines "curmudgeon" as a crusty, ill-tempered old man. That seems unduly harsh to me. I much prefer the definition offered by Jon Winokur in his book *The Portable Curmudgeon,* a delightful compendium of quotations and anecdotes from H. L. Mencken, Groucho Marx, Mark Twain, and a host of other world-class grumps. According to Winokur, a curmudgeon is "anyone who hates hypocrisy and pretense and has the temerity to say so; anyone with the habit of pointing out unpleasant facts in an engaging and humorous manner." That's the sort of curmudgeonliness I aspire to, though like Ben, there are times when I'm just plain grumpy, but hey, even the relentlessly cheerful can have a bad day.

Two other things had Ben shaking his head that day. His attempt at buying a shirt for his son-in-law, Bob, Shirley's husband, had apparently not gone well, and he resolved that thenceforth Bob could buy his own. Most of the head-shaking, though, was reserved for my parents and their spendthrift ways. To hear Ben tell it, the house Dad was fixing up—the house we would soon move into—was an exercise in manorial excess, or to use today's term for real estate costing more than its worth: sure to be underwater. In truth, it was a modest five-room house with a living room, dining room, and kitchen down, and two bedrooms up. There was only one bathroom. There was no garage, necessitating that the family vehicles be parked on the street. Wintertime street parking in Minnesota would never be counted as a luxury by the lord of any manor, nor is a new furnace ever thought to be an excess in these frosty latitudes. And don't forget those POW bunk beds.

Ben had lived through the Great Depression and he probably thought that gave him license to cluck about his son's spending, but it does seem a bit disingenuous in light of the house he would build seven years later, in 1955, the house where I now live. Not that it qualifies as a manor either, but it is roomy, and its roofline, wide eaves, and grouped windows reflect the architectural influence of Frank Lloyd Wright that was popular at the time. It's well built too, thanks in part to it being a Warner Brothers production, but also because Ben spent the entire construction period peering closely over the Warners' shoulders. Each time a load of lumber arrived on-site, Ben reportedly climbed onto the truck to survey the knots. If the knot count exceeded the permissible level—a number determined by Ben—the load was rejected.

Over its nearly sixty-year life span, the house has seen numerous upgrades and even an addition to the master bedroom when Pat and I moved in, but never has there been a need to remedy flaws in the original workmanship. Much of that original workmanship still stands out, like the pink glazed tile bathroom that fairly shouts "1950s!" The reason we did the master bedroom addition was so we could add a master bath and not have to rely on that pink place. The pink place has grown on us, though, and we have no plans for changing it. We've come to think of it as retro-chic.

Another surviving original feature of the house is the living and dining room carpet. If the only idea to be conveyed is that the floor is covered, then it would suffice to say there's a rug and leave it at that, but such a generic statement would never do for an unrepentant name-dropper like Ben. If he bought a prestigious product, he wanted folks to know about it, so he took great delight in letting it be known that he had Taj Mahal carpeting. As brand names go, Taj Mahal surely implies quality, but Ben didn't stop there. He also took every opportunity to repeat the manufacturer's claim that the carpet would last three generations. And that brings us to the moment of truth, to the place where the rubber meets the road, for I am the third generation, the person best qualified to judge the veracity of that claim. So does Taj Mahal carpet really last three generations? Absolutely—so long as you don't walk on it. In untrodden spots behind furniture and in corners the stuff is like new, but in a heavily traveled hallway it didn't last a single generation and was replaced by my parents. The rest of it is still there, but it's fairly worn, and if Pat has her way it'll be gone before this book reaches publication. Still, sixty years is a pretty good run for a rug, and that pink glazed tile will likely last a thousand. All and all, Ben built himself a fine house.

CHAPTER 12

FOOD, GLORIOUS FOOD!

June 10, Hotel Bristol, Oslo

My own dearest Ben,

Well, here we are in Norway—have been here a day but didn't get a chance to write yesterday. Almost got up a 2 o'clock to write you; had gotten to bed at 12 but didn't go to sleep—seeing too many people, drinking too much coffee and tea, and it wasn't dark either, sort of twilight at 12. I could see my watch to tell the time, and it kept getting lighter, but most of all I was so lonely for you. I lay there thinking of you and wishing I were home with you. I just don't know how I can take it much longer, and here only half the time has gone. Two weeks ago today I left, but it does seem such a long time. I'll certainly never do it again. Am enjoying everything and seeing so much of interest, but it is too long a time to be away so far from you. Your letter was waiting for me here, and I was so happy to hear from you. Am sorry my letters take so long to get to you, but hope you have gotten some by now. I was disappointed not to get your London letter when I got here, as I had left this as a forwarding address. Will have to call the hotel in London when I get back. I suppose my next London letter will be the last I'll get, but I will be so happy to be on my way back to you. I got a letter from Fritzie yesterday—was so glad to hear from her. I miss Fritzie, Charles and the children, and would like to be home when they are living there. Am glad they are there to look after you too.

To go back to Mon. morning when I wrote you at Copenhagen—it was a beautiful day, first one we'd had. In the morning we wandered over the town, we could take only one tour—one was cancelled because of gas rationing. We enjoyed our walk over to the Town Hall Square, went through the fish market, not far from the king's palace and parliament. Over at the square we sat and watched children feeding pigeons, etc. We enquired for a good place to eat, and were sent to the swankiest place in town. It was lovely in there, and here we only wanted a sandwich. I did order fruit salad, and it was served on a slice of bread as a sandwich. That's the way they make them here—sandwiches I mean—a lot of junk on a piece of bread, which you eat with knife and fork. I miss fruit and vegetables, tho we get some. Haven't had much meat since I left home, but don't miss it too much. Our tour over the city was nice, but we didn't see cathedrals as in other cities. One church built in the shape of a pipe organ was very beautiful and modern. I sat with a WAC on leave from Berlin who was interesting. The main point of interest seemed to be the big brewery they took us through. Showed us the huge tanks it was brewed in, the storage cellars where it is aged for 8 months, which is supposed to give it extra bouquet. We saw the filling, capping and labeling machines, which made me think of home. I wished you could be there to see it. They took us up to a big hall where there were tables filled with lager and pilsner beer, and everyone told to drink all they could, so we had to sit there while some drank 4 bottles. They had orange squash for us non-beer drinkers, so I broke down and had a bottle of that.

We had dinner that night at the sidewalk café at our hotel. There was quite a lot of traffic, I never saw so many bicycles in my life. They come up the street in swarms. There are over 400,000 in the city, everyone from 3 year olds to grandparents ride on bikes and they carry all sorts of loads on them. We decided to go out to Tivoli that evening, it's a famous amusement park. It is laid out like a park—beautiful flowers and fountains. In one building they were having a symphony orchestra concert. We just looked in and went over to the "Pike"—all the things like rollercoasters and Ferris wheels, old mill games of chance and shooting galleries, dance halls and many attractive places to eat. What made it so nice was there were no barkers, so the whole atmosphere was pleasant and enjoyable. We just walked through it all, and then back to bed as we had to get up at 6 in the morning to take the 8 o'clock for Oslo. On the train we were in a large compartment with a seat for 3 at either end and 4 easy chairs and table in between. We had interesting traveling companions that day. A couple from Holland who could speak English, a Swedish gal who is coming to Minnesota to write articles for a magazine. We had a lovely trip up the coast of Denmark and ferried across to Sweden. We rode thru Sweden most of the afternoon. We had quite a time with our meals on the train. We started out in Denmark and had a little Danish money left, but they wouldn't accept it for lunch as we were in Sweden, so I cashed $5 to pay for lunch. Then for supper we were in Norway and I thought I'd have to cash another bill, but fortunately had enough left of Swedish money, and they would take that. It seems Danish and Norwegian crowns aren't rated quite as high as Swedish. Here I got 49 crowns for $10. In Sweden it was a little over 3 to $1.

The scenery in Norway is really beautiful, and it was a lovely sight as we came into Oslo. Tues. evening we came to the hotel where we had a call from Kristine wanting us to come out. We cleaned up a bit and took a taxi out to see her. Enjoyed a visit with her and her husband—we like them both so much. We got home and to bed at 11:30 and were up early to go over town to get reservations at a Bergen hotel, also railroad tickets for Friday morning—hope we can get in a hotel. Right across from the travel agency I saw a sign "Rolf Bordewich Jensen," so decided it must be Harold's cousin. There were so many Odd Jensens in the phone book, I wasn't going to call, but as we were right there we went in. Odd wasn't there but his younger brother was. He was very nice to us, served us tea in his office and said he wanted to take us around today, but we didn't feel we should put him through the bother. We did a little shopping, it started to rain, so we came back to the hotel to get a taxi out to Kristine's again, as we were invited for dinner at 3:30. The usual dinner time here is 4:00, but her husband has to go to the Storthing, so they eat early. We had a good dinner, tasted the best I've had, even had roast veal, which her son had sent her. We felt guilty eating any of it, but it was so good. After dinner her husband took us to a beautiful park nearby, and a beautiful view of the city. A Minnesota car was parked outside, but we didn't see the owner. On our way back we stopped to see a relative who lived nearby. She insisted on having us for lunch, then she went with us back to Kristine's for what they call coffee, which they always have at 6 o'clock—rolls, cakes and coffee. Some of Kristine's relatives were there so we had quite a party. They mostly speak English so we don't have much trouble. Bertha is getting quite a talker in Norwegian, but I don't try it. We left there about 9 and stopped to call on another relative who lives nearby. She is a French teacher and speaks very good English. She also insisted on feeding us, so we eat often, but not so much when we eat. I haven't had too much of an appetite over here. I always seem to lose my appetite when I have to eat at hotels for very long. This home cooking here does taste good even if they can't get much to do with. They gave us ration cards in Denmark and Sweden and here, and we hope to have quite a bit of ours to turn over to our relatives. At 11 o'clock we started for home, and these two ladies walked a ways with us to show us where Leo's dental friends were located, as one of them was the dentist for my relative. We enjoyed the walk so much—still daylight and so many on the streets. I should think the folks wouldn't get enough sleep here in summer, but s'pose they make up for it in winter when they get about 3 hours of daylight. I went right to bed, listening to strains of music down below in the restaurant. Much of it was good American music, and the last songs the crowd joined in singing in English—"On a bicycle built for two" and "My Bonnie lies over the ocean." Sounded good.

This morning I am staying in the room till late. Bertha and Leo have had breakfast and have gone over to the travel bureau, and then are going to call on Leo's dentist friends, and the highway engineer, a friend of Mr. Kipps. We were invited out to Kristine's for dinner today too, but are just going out for coffee at 6 o'clock. It's a beautiful day out and we plan to take a trip to a high point above the city where we will get a beautiful view. There is a hotel there, so we plan to eat there.

We will probably be in Bergen a day or so, then to Odda and Skudenes and on to Stavanger. Am getting anxious to be homeward bound. Was glad to get Shirley's letter—she does always seem to be in a whirl, doesn't she? I seem to have gotten rid of some bug which I picked up—didn't feel too good when we left Brussels, but took some aspirin, and slept a lot on the train, and managed to lose that achy feeling, and feel fine again. I try to get in all the rest I can. Hope you continue to feel fine. Am always thinking of you and missing you. I love you so much, it is so hard to be away from you. About 22 more days—a long time.

All my love, Clara

Clara's stay in Copenhagen was brief, though they did manage to take in Tivoli Gardens. I haven't been to Copenhagen, but I understand that skipping Tivoli Gardens would be tantamount to visiting Orlando and not going to Disney World. She did seem a bit disappointed that their tour of the city failed to include a cathedral. Apparently after visiting cathedrals in London, Paris, and Brussels she wasn't yet cathedraled-out, and the tour's high point—a brewery—proved a poor substitute. The brewery's filling and capping and labeling of beer bottles did remind her of a similar process at the Olivia Canning Company, but those thoughts of home were overshadowed by having to wait in the sample room while the tour's beer drinkers downed up to four bottles each. When I travel I'm more likely to take the view that having seen one cathedral, I've seen them all but that each brewery is a new day in itself. I suppose that reveals my cultural shortcomings, though I'm fairly sure that had Ben been there he'd have opted for a good Danish lager or pilsner over an orange squash.

Clara's letters so far have dwelled more on her lack of appetite than on reports of fine dining, but now our travelers have reached Norway, the Motherland, which abounds with cousins who are determined to feed their guests a meal every hour or so. What makes all this feasting all the more generous is that it happens against a backdrop of food rationing, still in force three years after the end of World War II.

The thought of generosity amid hardship brought on by war calls to mind another act of remarkable generosity, one played out on a national level: the Marshall Plan. General George Marshall was the U.S. Army's chief of staff during World War II. He was a warrior's warrior, but with the war's end President Truman named him secretary of state, and in that role he devised the plan to spend vast amounts of American treasure to rebuild Europe. Never before had a victorious nation shown such magnanimity to those ravaged by war, ally and enemy alike. It's fitting that such a plan be named for a warrior turned diplomat, and it earned Marshall the Nobel Peace Prize. As a nation we lose our way from time to time, but when it really counts we seem to find our better angels. The Marshall Plan was perhaps our finest hour.

But now it's back to Norway where, in the time it took to read the last paragraph, another meal has undoubtedly been laid on the table. It's good that Clara has her appetite back as I've always associated her with culinary treats, especially those that delight a child's palate. In an earlier chapter I promised more detail on Clara's cornucopia of sweets, and now I shall make good on that.

To begin with, Clara's catering to kid tastes wasn't simply a matter of keeping a bunch of candy around. That would have been too easy. No, most of her treats came by way of her cooking, as with her already mentioned pancakes, drenched in maple syrup. At times the kids got to participate in the process, as we did when Clara decided that a taffy pull was needed to while away an hour or so. Her Christmas cookies were the best, especially her spritz, which literally melted in the mouth. The whole family still uses her recipe.

She was the only person I've ever known to make an entire meal out of strawberry shortcake, one of her favorite summer lunch menus. When shortcake was just for dessert, Clara might design to serve it with store-bought whipped cream squirted from a can, but when it was the complete meal she insisted on whole cream as the road to better nutrition. Cholesterol, shmolesterol, that was a lunch!

And she was resourceful, making magic out of whatever happened to be at hand. Visit her in her garden on a summer day and you might well find yourself holding a stalk of rhubarb, made tastier by dipping it in the small cup of sugar that suddenly appeared. But my all-time favorite—the perfect kid treat for any time of day, any time of year—was one of Clara's brown sugar sandwiches. Start with a single slice of white bread. Spread a film of butter on one side to add richness and also to act as mortar to bond the sugar to the bread. Then, layer on the brown sugar to a depth of, say, an eighth of an inch, and you've got a treat guaranteed to put a smile on any kid's face and drive any dentist to fits of apoplexy.

Okay, so the foods I've just described might not be the healthiest, but that's not to say that I didn't encounter my share of vegetables and gag food in my growing-up diet. I certainly did, though that was my mother's responsibility. Clara took a grandmother's prerogative, but there was more to it than simply feeding a sweet tooth. All those wonderful aromas and flavors coming from her kitchen were suffused with love, and that made it all the more sweet.

A final thought on Clara's letter: she notes that cousin Kristine's husband went regularly to the Storthing, which is Norway's parliament. No mention is made as to whether the husband was an elected representative or a non-elected public official. We aren't even told his name, and extensive family-tree research goes beyond the scope of this work; still, it's nice to know that public service can be traced in my family back to the old country. Ben and my dad and I all served in elected office in Olivia, not in positions of great importance, but positions that brought a sense of satisfaction nonetheless.

CHAPTER 13

WHAT'S IN A NAME?

Monday, June 7

Dearest Clara,

Was so glad to get your letters. Got two of them Saturday morning—from London and Paris—and then Charles brought the one from Brussels out to the lake yesterday. You really seem to be seeing things, but from the sound of your letters you seem rather tired and are doing too much. Better slow down a little. S'pose you won't have to go quite so fast and furious when you get to Norway. Was really surprised when you told about going to the Folies Bergere. The kids got quite a kick out of it. Told them that if I had been along you probably wouldn't have let me go. Am glad you went as now you know what it is when you hear of the Folies Bergere. We also got quite a kick out of you and Leo having a bottle of wine and he feeling dizzy all afternoon. The kids thought you were getting to be quite frisky. What does Bertha do, just go thirsty?

Got rid of the auditor Saturday afternoon about 3:00. We were down here until twelve Friday nite and back again at 7:00 the next morning. He was anxious to get thru and get back to

Minneapolis early Saturday. After that I got a few things to eat and went out to the lake. Gunder and family were out there. Cooked a steak but didn't feel much like work so just loafed. The grass was so dry Saturday that I didn't mow it. Yesterday I got up late and then decided I had better shellac the trim around all the windows and doors. Was rather a slow job, but got along nicely until Charles and Fritzie showed up with the kids, and they weren't much help. Had things moved all over the cottage, but finally got finished about 5:00, put things back and then Fritzie got a lunch. Guess she was all for going home earlier as the kids were cranky. Had supper and then they stayed till dark. I decided to stay out there. Listened to the radio and read until about 10:30 and then rolled in and slept till about 8:00 this morning. It rained quite hard for a while yesterday afternoon so decided this morning to mow part of the lawn before coming in, so didn't get in until about 10:00.

Haven't been down to the house yet. Guess Charles is down to his place. The plasterers got thru there Saturday so guess the next thing will be paper hanging and painting. If he does all the painting himself it will probably be quite a while before they are ready to move in. Schullers were up to the cottage Saturday afternoon. Invited me down to Sunday dinner but didn't know when the kids would be out. Wound up eating a hamburger sandwich with Hoaglunds so didn't do too much cooking myself yesterday. Weren't very many out. Andersons were there and Hoaglunds had company in the afternoon. Guess Jacobsons went into the city for a birthday party for young Harry. Gunder said Neil Wagemakers were there in the afternoon and he was looking at Bunker's lot and said he was going in to see him today. He will probably buy it and said if he did he would like to move the fence to the west side of that lot.

Really not much to write about as I haven't been anywhere except the office and the lake. I do miss you a lot and it isn't the same anywhere without you. Someone remarked the other day, guess it was Gunder, that I acted out at the lake as if I didn't know what to do with myself. Everyone is getting along fine here. Fritzie feeds me most of the time and does my washing when she can get the clothes. The kids are fine most of the time and are not cranky too much. Chuckie said at the lake yesterday, "Bopa, I want to go with you." I asked him where we should go and he said, "Someplace." He seems to have taken quite a shine to me.

Had a little rain here Friday P.M. but not enough to soak in any. The farmers are certainly beginning to holler and already think they aren't going to get any crops. About time to eat so guess I had better get started home as Fritzie is quite prompt about her meals. See everything you can but don't go at it too hard as we don't want you all tired out when you get back. Am missing you and thinking of you and loving you all the time. Take care of yourself.

All my love, Ben

Ben poked a little fun at his teetotaler sister-in-law when he wondered if Bertha just goes thirsty. One senses a bit of mutual disapproval between the two of them, and perhaps that, and not the demands of business, was Ben's chief reason for not going along on the trip.

Yes, they called me Chuckie. I suppose I looked like a Chuckie in 1948, but I don't anymore and now folks simply call me Chuck. No one in the family has ever called me by my given name, which is Charles, because it was always necessary to distinguish me from my father, who was called Charles his whole life, even as a little tyke.

I've never liked being a junior. It's always struck me as odd that people would give a name to a boy, presumably because they liked it, and then never call him by it. They don't do that to girls. Have you ever heard of a Sally Jr. or, God forbid, Agnes Jr.? My parents should have seen this coming. My mother's brother Arthur Jr. was called Bud; her cousin Eric Jr., Babe. Further complicating matters, Mother's Uncle Eric—the one responsible for Babe—took to assigning nicknames for no apparent reason. Arthur Jr., known to one and all as Bud, was rechristened Hank by Eric, and then to further muddy the waters, Eric also dubbed me Hank. Why is a two-Charles family not permitted when a two-Hank one is? And giving me the added handle of Hank accomplished nothing. Going from Chuck to Hank is what the business world calls a lateral move; it neither promotes nor demotes, though admittedly Hank is an improvement over Chuckie. But Uncle Eric also nicknamed my mother, and there I think he was onto something.

Mother was born a poor preacher's kid in a tiny tumbleweed town in western South Dakota, not a silver-spoon beginning by any stretch. She was christened LaVerne, a perfectly good name, but one that failed to capture the totality of the person. She was gorgeous, smart, and musically talented—all qualities a LaVerne might well possess—but there was something more, something hard to define. For lack of a better word, she was distinctive. She had style. She liked a good time, and sparks seemed to follow in her wake. There was a sense of grace about her. Uncle Eric apparently recognized early on that the name LaVerne didn't tell the whole story, so he gave her a nickname that did: Fritzie.

Despite all her vivacity and grace, Mother had a chip on her shoulder, a chip most likely rooted in her humble beginnings. That chip only got bigger when she married into a family where everyone else—her husband, her mother-in-law, her father-in-law, her sister-in-law, her brother-in-law—had college degrees. She didn't resent those degrees, but she wasn't going to live in their shadows either. It was as if she said, "College, huh? Well, catch a look at me!" She also became the family grammarian, taking special delight in correcting her college-educated children.

Her scrutiny of my efforts with the English language rose to a new level when, after a career in business, I sought a writer's life. Not that she was overly critical of my work. Quite the contrary, but then she always viewed anything done by anyone in her family to be beyond reproach, and she embraced my scribbling with the same enthusiasm. She did, however, take exception with the vulgar language used by some of my characters from time to time. I pointed out, of course, that the vulgarities appeared in dialogue, not in the narrative, and were necessary to the development of the characters. After all, if you're trying to depict a truly coarse or profane person, then "by golly" or "gosh darn" just won't get the job done. She didn't buy it. Wagging her finger, she reminded me that, "You're judged by the company you keep."

A YOUTHFUL FRITZIE.

Dad and Mother proved the axiom that opposites attract, and the subject on which they were polar opposites was exercise. It's already been noted that my dad was an accomplished athlete, and as such he viewed exercise as a cure for everything. Mother, on the other hand, subscribed to the theory that each heart has a predetermined number of beats, so there is nothing to be gained and much to be lost by hurrying the process along. This argument went on for most of their married life, with Dad extolling sweat and Mother rolling her eyes at the very thought. But when advancing years began impacting her life, Dad finally convinced her to give exercise a try. She still had no intention of sweating, perhaps a ladylike glow, but first things first. Before there could be any workouts, the sartorial needs of exercise had to be met—style, always style—so Mother went out and bought two fashionable exercise outfits, and only then did she undertake her first workout. It consisted of a walk around the block, after which she decreed an end to such foolishness and never exercised again, so if you're keeping track you will note that she had twice as many workout outfits as workouts. And she outlived Dad by eleven years.

In many ways she thought herself a brand, and like anyone who owns a brand she sought to keep it in good light. The material symbols of her brand were gold shoes—she owned about ten pairs—and clothing made in a leopard pattern. Mostly, though, the brand was about her grace and vivacity. That became harder to maintain in her last years as the maladies of old age piled on, and yes, she had her share of complaints, but mostly she saved those for Judy and me. Everyone else got her A-game. Right up to the end she would get up every morning—even the days she didn't want to—put on her makeup, and roll out her brand. A woman like that ought to be called Fritzie.

CHAPTER 14

BEAUTY

Odda, Norway, Monday June 14

My dearest Ben,

I wish so you could be here with me in this very beautiful place—it is overwhelming. Here I sit on the porch of my cousin's home, high mountains on all sides, and situated on what is practically an island in the fjord. You can well know how I like this place. The mountains to the left are so high they are snow-capped with glaciers on the sides. Streams from the melting snow come tumbling down the mountainside. On all sides of us are waterfalls that I can hear as I go to sleep. The scenery we saw on the way over here is the most beautiful and awe inspiring I've ever seen. Always the high mountains on all sides, hundreds of waterfalls, many quite large, and the fjords. All roads follow the fjords. These roads are very difficult to build, mostly being blasted from solid rock. They are not too wide, and at times yesterday when we met a car or bus our bus had to maneuver to just barely squeeze past. I can see why they don't have so many cars here in Norway.

It is hard to keep track of the days here, they are all the same, but I am sure it was Thursday morning I last wrote you. I would write oftener but it is hard when we are on the go all the time. I am always thinking of you and missing you so. Am glad the time is over half gone, and when we put our watches ahead one hour in Sweden I felt like we were homeward bound and that much nearer to you. I am glad to be going westward again. It is too long a time to be away from you. They all say I should bring you too. This trip is wonderful, and I am enjoying it, but never again will I go without you.

To go back to Thursday morning, Bertha and Leo called on the highway dept. chief with a letter from Mr. Kipp who had taken him around when he was in Minnesota, so he wanted to take us around Norway. They called for me at the hotel and we drove up to a high place on the mountain where we had a beautiful view of Oslo and the fjord. We had lunch up there at tables out on the terrace—of course I liked that—then he took us around the city to a museum where they had some Viking ships from the year 1,000. We also saw the *Fram*, the ship in which Nansen and Amundsen went to the north and south poles. He wanted to show us more, but we were going back to Kristine's for coffee, so we had to go back to the hotel. We did a bit of shopping while Leo called on his dentist friends. We enjoyed our visit with Kristine and stayed with her until her husband came home from the Storthing, which meets evenings. We walked back to the hotel and to bed by 11 as we were leaving early next morning for Bergen. It was a beautiful trip over on the train—a lady who manages a magazine in Oslo was in our compartment and interesting to talk to. We climbed until we were up 4,000 ft. in the mountains, thru hundreds of tunnels. At the highest point there was no vegetation, only snow. We stopped at many mountain villages where everyone got off the train for 10 to 20 minutes. Most of the people went into cafes to buy sandwiches. We had our lunch on the train, but bought sandwiches for supper.

We left Oslo about 8:45 and arrived at Bergen about 9:30 that evening. Of course we didn't have reservations at the hotel. We did have the agent in Oslo get our tickets and hotel reservations the day before, but on such short notice we couldn't get into one of the best hotels, as we have been doing. We were glad to get any place to stay, and the place we stayed was small but clean. Only a wash bowl in the room, running water, of course, and a telephone so it wasn't too bad to have to go down the hall to the toilet, and we dispensed with a bath. We had something to eat, then right to bed and to sleep. Have been waking rather early as most of the time we are leaving early for a train, etc. I was counting up last night and find I've slept in 11 different places since leaving home. I seem to be standing it all pretty well. Of course there is a lot of sitting, so I shouldn't get too tired.

At Bergen we roamed around the town in the morning and then my cousin Kirsten—who teaches art at the Bergen high school—called for us and took us to her home for lunch. Her mother, father and brother Karl were there—they are so nice— and so nice to see. We liked them all so much. Her father has been in Minnesota and his cousin is married to Leo's real estate agent. A small world it is. Kirsten and her mother took us out to Slettebaaken where my grandmother Barbara Ruud was born. We were so thrilled with the place, the house part way up a mountain overlooking Bergen and the fjord. Bergen is surrounded by 7 mountains. This home is over 200 years old and still looks like it will last for many years. The brass hardware, the tile roof, the windows, the original wallpaper— which is hand painted—the old stove (oven as they call it) are all so marvelous. The architecture is very similar to what we have today. I hope the pictures Leo took will be good.

That evening we walked out along the docks. The Stavangerfjord had just docked, so we watched the people go on board. We saw some evidences of bombing along the harbor, then we went back to the hotel and to bed by daylight. It seems so queer to have it light all night long. We were up early on Sunday and down to the bus depot. Kirsten and Karl were down to see us off. We've had beautiful sunny days in Norway and are so glad to have sun again. We left Bergen at 8:30 and got here about 4 o'clock. We had to change buses 3 times and had a short ferry across the fjord, which we enjoyed. Our cousin Otto was there to meet us with 2 of his children and took us to his mother's for coffee. She is widow of our cousin. Otto's wife and baby came too, as well as his sister and her son. We like them all so well and they make us feel most welcome. We went to Otto's home for supper—he lives up quite high with a lovely view over the city and fjord. Bertha and Leo stayed there last night, and I came out to his sister's. Her husband has a factory and I met him last night. They have two sons—one left yesterday for a year's military training. Most everyone speaks some English so we get along very well. I slept late this morning. It seems so good to be in a home. I've had breakfast and here I sit like a lady of leisure, wishing you were here with me. Give my love to the family. I miss them all, but I am desolate without you. I love you so much. Tomorrow we go to Skudenes where my mother lived.

All my love, Clara

P.S. Will you keep my letters—I am behind on my diary and may forget some.

I'm thankful for Clara's postscript, for if the letters hadn't been saved I would now likely be working on another satirical novel. Not that that would be a bad thing, but I'm having a lot more fun with this project than I expected—hope my enjoyment shines through the writing. I suspect Ben would have saved the letters even without the postscript, as that was just something people used to do. Today we don't write letters in the first place, much less save them. I did pause to wonder, though, if Clara might have hesitated to save her personal letters had she known that her own grandson would have the temerity to hang them out for all to see. Oh, well, I've already crossed that bridge.

Leo was most likely a fine dentist, but Clara seems unsure of his skill as a photographer. This isn't the first letter in which she voiced some doubt over whether Leo's camera will do justice to all they are seeing. And if this letter is any indication, they were seeing some pretty spectacular sights.

Clara's rhapsodic descriptions of Norway's natural beauty also caused me to wonder why her parents had ever left, and for Iowa of all places. Let me hasten to add that I intend no slight to my worthy neighbors to the south—the Hawkeyes football team not withstanding—but in truth Iowa lacks Norway's majesty. It doesn't have beautiful fjords ringed with snow-capped mountains and waterfalls tumbling down everywhere. But my great-grandparents' decision to emigrate was surely about more than scenery, and the Norway of the nineteenth century was surely different from the Norway of 1948, just as it was most certainly different from the oil-rich, progressive democracy we know today.

Indeed, Norway has had a tough history. The country was subjugated, first by Denmark, then by Sweden, warring nations that reduced the Norwegians to pawn status and dragged them into war after war after war. In addition to suffering wars Norway also endured plague and famine and the whimsy of kings. In short, Norway wasn't exempt from Europe's long bloody history. By the middle of the nineteenth century folks had had enough, and they began emigrating in droves, mostly bound for the American Midwest. Clara's parents were part of that migration.

If you need to escape a place where life is hard, it's good to have a destination where opportunity beckons. Luckily, the middle of the nineteenth century saw the United States expanding westward, opening rich land for homesteading. It should be noted here that not everyone, specifically Native Americans, saw great opportunity in that westward expansion, but that's another story. This one is about Norwegians seeking a new life. As to the scenery, it stands to reason that the most majestic places on Earth—think Norway—can be hard to farm, while more boring landscapes—think Iowa—offer some of the most fertile land in the world.

And so they came, drawn by the promise of good land, political stability, and the rule of law. They were "your tired, your poor, your huddled masses yearning to breathe free" of the famous poem by Emma Lazarus. If that doesn't qualify as beauty, then I don't know what beauty is.

CHAPTER 15

GETTING GRANDPA'S GOAT

Thursday evening, June 10

Dearest Clara,

Got your letter today from Brussels. Certainly made good time as you wrote it Monday morning. Sounds like you don't feel too good and hope you haven't been over doing it. Better take it easy and not come home all tired out. Sounds however as though you were enjoying yourself and are seeing a lot.

Just came home from the clubhouse. Had a mixed tournament out there tonight and everyone was asking about you. Agnes said she hoped you were keeping a diary as she would want to hear all about it when you get back. Just three weeks ago today since you left and it seems a lot longer than that. Will be so glad when you get back home. Didn't play with any women tonight as there were none when we started out so had a foursome of men. Didn't do too good. Had a 43. Pretty good crowd out there and a very good dinner—Swiss steak. Wish that we were getting some of the rain you are getting. Have to keep the sprinklers going practically all day and it keeps one busy taking care of them. Your plants east of the house are still alive and I gave them some water today so should be okay. Also watered your flower bed as it was too dry for the seeds to sprout. Looks like a bum year so far, but maybe things will change. Haven't done too much since writing you Monday. Tuesday went out to men's night. Played 9 holes for a 44, which wasn't too good. Not many out, so guess there isn't too much interest. Charles was chairman of the committee and served beans and bologna so sort of stole my thunder. Glad I'm not president anymore. The bottle cooler went on the blink and the refrigerator also went haywire. Noticed tonight that they had another refrigerator, a used one. Yesterday I drove up to Willmar to get the car checked over on the first 1,000 mile check. Didn't want anyone here to do it. Have finally managed to get 1,000 miles on it though I haven't been any place. Just out to the lake and around town.

Charles is busy now getting his woodwork painted, which will probably take him quite a while. I still think they will probably still be at our place when you get back, though I guess they have company coming in July so will probably try to get moved as soon as they can. Am getting along fine with them at home, though the kids get my goat once in a while. Judy is a little devil at times and seems like she has gotten so she cries quite readily.

Saw Mehlhouses at the clubhouse and he was asking if I would be at the lake Sunday. Thought they would probably be out there in the afternoon. Haven't been out this week so will probably go out again Saturday. Fritzie said something about coming out to stay over Saturday night, but guess they will wait till Sunday as Charles will want to work at the house. Have been thinking of planting the window boxes, but am not sure just what you want to put in them. Tomorrow is Charles birthday, but haven't heard anything about any special doings. S'pose I should take them out to dinner. Thought some of taking them to Sacred Heart, and then thought it might be better to wait until you get back.

A couple of Minneapolis bankers were here Tuesday and stuck around a good share of the afternoon. Also had a letter from Brokmann saying that he and his wife will be thru here the 16th and wanted us to have lunch with them at the country club or some such place. I am afraid he is going to be disappointed. Started the boys trimming the shrubbery around the office today. Guess I could do it myself a lot faster but am not going to do it. Will also have to get busy on getting our equipment lined up for our cook shack. Have spotted a couple of gas ranges and may buy one of them. Fritzie was out to a shower last night and didn't get in until one. Said they played cards till about twelve. She still gets around. Guess she is driving to Willmar in the morning to do some shopping. Think I will send your watch with her over to Paffraft's.

They are coming down our street with curb and gutter now. Had Giffie down there last night and told him we wanted new walks put in. Hate to have the lawn torn up, but better to get it done while they are there if I can get him to do it. Am so glad to get your letters and look forward to them. Would much rather have you home however. Really seems such a long time since you left and we all miss you. When I left the house this morning I said goodbye Chuckie, and he says, "Goodbye, Grandfather." He is getting to be quite the talker, though it is hard to follow him at times. Take care of yourself and don't get too tired. We are all fine here and I got over the bum feeling that I had. Am missing you all the time so hurry home as soon as you can. Time I was getting to bed.

All my love, Ben

P.S. Enclosing another letter from Shirley. Will keep the picture of the piano here as it might make too much weight. The piano is a Story & Clark, Georgian Console.

P.S. Quite a difference in the spelling of some of the cities over there. Noticed that Brussels is Bruxelles and that Copenhagen on the postmark is Kobenhavn. You seem to get my letters however.

P.S. Judy said the other morning that her belly hurt. Fritzie was quite shocked and wondered where she had heard that. There is quite a gang of kids she plays with in the neighborhood.

Ben gets a bit carried away with postscripts on this letter. The first simply revealed that my aunt had acquired a piano and warrants no further comment. In the second he remarks on the odd spelling by the locals of the different cities Clara has visited, as if they ought to know better. Yet despite this Babel-like confusion, Ben noted that the mail somehow managed to get through. The third postscript had my mother shocked and wondering how the word "belly" found its way into my sister's vocabulary. Belly hardly qualifies as profanity, even in its mildest forms, but I suppose my mother thought it unladylike. Ben was probably right in blaming it on a gang of neighborhood kids. A few years later my own vocabulary was broadened—Mother thought coarsened—by the neighborhood rabble. Mother was right, of course, but that's not to say my new words were without merit, though admittedly they're more useful in novel writing than in a work such as this.

Ben reported on more golf outings. First he wrote about a mixed tournament where his foursome was unmixed due to a shortage of women. He deemed the Swiss steak to be very good and his score of forty-three to be not so good. He had also played on men's night the previous Tuesday, again expressing dissatisfaction with his score of forty-four. A word here on Ben's golf scores: he was fifty-eight years old at the time and both of those scores were sub-bogey rounds. When I played the game, that was about as good as I ever scored and usually I didn't do that well. True, Ben was an athlete, a college baseball player, but he didn't have a shelf full of golf trophies as my dad did, so I suspect the griping about his scores was a bit disingenuous. I'm not sure what to make of Ben's comment about my dad stealing his thunder by serving beans and bologna for men's night. Stealing thunder usually involves the claiming of bragging rights, but I don't see how that works here. There is the coarser possibility that he was referring to a different sort of thunder, the kind sometimes produced by a meal of beans and bologna, but we have no way of knowing that, so we won't go there.

While we are on the subject of golf, I must digress and relate another of my dad's odd proclivities. When I say he was something of a Nazi, I hasten to add that he wasn't a brute bent on world war and genocide. He was a Nazi only in that he was meticulous about record keeping. He kept track of everything. I witnessed this firsthand at the Olivia Canning Company where he accumulated piles and piles of paper documenting obscure data that far exceeded good accounting and manufacturing practices. He recorded useless numbers with the same zeal that had led him to fill my attic with useless junk, and this penchant for writing everything down slopped over into his personal life as well.

After his death, I was tasked with going through his desk and files to winnow out the useless, to separate the wheat from the chaff. As expected, it was mostly chaff, but in the course of my winnowing I came upon a collection of pocket-size notebooks. There were dozens of them and their recorded content spanned many years. I quickly deciphered that they had been used to document two distinct universes of information. The first was his weight. He weighed himself each day, then diligently recorded the date and weight in one of the notebooks. From time to time he would add margin notes such as "Milwaukee Canners Convention" to explain a sudden spike of several pounds.

The other notebooks contained his golf scores. Sometimes he would list only a nine-hole score; other times he would record two nine-hole scores followed by the eighteen-hole total. The notebooks were never labeled "Golf Scores" or made any other reference to the game of golf, but given his love of the game and the range of the numbers, they could be nothing other than golf scores. There was, however, one additional column of numbers on the right margin that took me a bit longer to figure out. Some were posted like the scores in black ink, others in red ink. It finally occurred to me that this column could be nothing other than his winnings (black ink) and losses (red ink). Perhaps the most poignant entry of all was his very last. It was posted a month or so before he died and recorded that, at the age of eighty-three, he had shot a forty-four and made a couple bucks. Not a bad last round.

Okay, now it's back to Ben's letter. Like some previous letters, this one is gossipy and jumps around a lot, but in reading between the lines a clear theme emerges: as much as Ben longs for Clara's return, he is equally eager for my family to move out of his house. This is the second letter in which he fusses about how long it's taking my dad to paint the woodwork in our new house, thereby delaying our move. For Clara he tried to put a good spin on things when he says that he is "getting along fine with them at home," but then he reveals the other side when he says that Judy and I get his goat once in a while. (A fair reading of the letter clearly shows my sister, the little devil, to be responsible for most of the goat-getting, but I won't press the point.) It's all quite reminiscent of the days just after the war when Ben and Clara's house filled with returning veterans along with their wives, toddlers, and babies. You'll recall that during that period Ben also spent a lot of time at the office.

CHAPTER 16

KODAK MOMENTS

Friday the 18th, Skudenes, Norway

My own dearest Ben,

Two weeks from today and I should be home with you, and how happy I'll be with you again. The time has been so long, and I've been so lonely for you. I was so glad to get your letter yesterday, as I hadn't hoped for any more letters in Norway, as we didn't know just where we would be. They forwarded two letters from Oslo; one was waiting for me when we got here. I have all your letters except the one to London, and hope to get that when we get to London.

We had such a nice visit in Odda, where we stayed with 2nd cousins. I stayed at a different home than Bertha and Leo, but we had many meals together. We were in Odda from Sunday afternoon till Tuesday morning when we took a bus to a place near here, and a beautiful ride through the mountains. Our only 1st cousin, Agnes, met us with a taxi about 1 o'clock and we came to her place on an island upon which are 6 towns. One of them is Skudenes, the town where my mother was born. It is a quaint little fishing village—narrow streets leading every which way, houses built close together and facing most any direction. Agnes's home is right next to the one where my mother was born, and the people who live there let us come in and see the house. It's almost 200 years old, but still seems in good condition and still looks attractive. It is hard to believe. I have wished since coming to Norway that I had brought my Kodak.

They are a most kindly folk here, and since they knew the Americans were coming they have bought food and other things hard to get, and we surely have feasted while here. Seems like all we do is eat, so I am sure I have gained what I have lost and maybe more. I had lost quite a bit of weight—you know how I lose my appetite when I eat away from home for any length of time—so I hadn't been eating too much. Also when I had a touch of flu in Belgium I didn't eat much, so had lost a lot, but now my appetite is back again—such good food, and unusual food—so I am eating a lot. Agnes has had folks in here, and we've been invited out a lot, and we've met so many folks distantly related to us—mostly about 3rd cousins. They are all so nice, and it's been fun to meet them.

Yesterday a man took us in a boat out to the light house. We went to the top of it and had a wonderful view of the North Sea and the island here which seems mostly a mass of rocks. It really was a grand sight. We went past a liberty ship which went on the rocks last fall and broke in two. Yesterday the girl I stayed with in Odda came here to visit. She is Agnes's niece and talks English very well. Agnes talks English pretty well too, so we get along fine. Leo finds men to talk to who can speak English. He is promising everyone that they needn't worry about Russia, as Marshall won't let them do any harm.

We have met a few folks who were pupils of my mother when she taught school here. This afternoon we are going to take a ride around the island, and then for dinner at a 2nd cousins. Tomorrow we take a boat for Stavanger where we take a boat for New Castle. The North Sea can be pretty rough, but I'm hoping for smooth sailing. It is cool here, but has been sunny. Right now I am sitting in the sun, in a deck chair out on the patio and the sun surely feels good. Was glad to get Shirley's letter, also glad to have one from Faye with a bit of town news. Am counting the days till I get home. I love you so and miss you so.

All my love, Clara

A comment here about the sequencing of Ben and Clara's letters. You might have noticed that they don't always appear in chronological order. The problem, of course, is the lag time built into 1948 connectivity, which bears little resemblance to the connectivity of the twenty-first century. Clara still hadn't gotten the letter Ben sent to London, and they never are responding to the other's most recent letter. These lag-time issues would simply disappear if only Ben and Clara had laptops or smartphone, though it's probably best that they didn't, for if they'd had that technology it's likely that I wouldn't now have their letters on which to base this book. At any rate, I thought it best to ignore the dates and simply alternate the letters by writer, which I trust will be agreeable to most readers, save the real sticklers for detail among us.

Clara reports that Leo is telling all who will listen "that they needn't worry about Russia, as Marshall won't let them do any harm." Praise for George Marshall was sung in a previous chapter, but it does seem odd that Leo would single him out as our sole line of defense. What about Harry Truman? He was, after all, still president of the United

States, a job that comes with considerable power and authority. Leo's comment was most likely some rock-ribbed Republicanism showing through, and Truman was quite unpopular in some quarters in the summer of 1948. Boy, did Give 'em Hell Harry ever have a surprise in store for many folks come November.

In awe of all she has seen in Norway, Clara wished that she had brought her Kodak along. For the younger readers who might think cameras exist only as an ancillary function of cell phones, I take this opportunity to explain that Clara's Kodak was a handheld device (to use a twenty-first-century term) whose sole function was taking pictures. Yes, it was a camera, and an inexpensive one, at that. It was manufactured and sold by the good folks at Eastman Kodak for what was surely a modest profit, but it got their foot in Clara's door, for if she wanted to use her Kodak, she was obliged to buy the film that Eastman Kodak also happened to sell. For the younger readers I won't bother trying to explain what film is; just know that in all likelihood it sold at a better profit margin than the camera.

And that brings us back to the comparison of twenty-first-century connectivity with what passed for connectivity in 1948. Ben and Clara's lagged-time letters are filled with wondering and imagining about what the other was doing, not to mention wondering if Leo's photos will turn out. Today's gadgetry eliminates the need for that sort of wondering and imagining. People at the opposite ends of the earth can instantly communicate with one another. Pictures taken are viewed instantly and just as quickly transmitted elsewhere.

All this connectedness is here to stay and will surely increase with added innovation, but that's not to say there are no minuses to go with the plusses. The elimination of lag time in passing along information is certainly a positive, and it is well argued that social media have a democratizing effect on the world by exposing the Big Lies of tyrants. On the other hand, social media can also facilitate the telling of small lies, and we do look rather silly wandering through life with our eyes fixed on our phones. Beyond mere appearances, though, I sometimes fear that we are connected to the point of distraction, to the point where creativity is impaired.

Pat and I are as gadget-connected as most, certainly in our age group, though admittedly that's usually a matter of her leading the way and pulling me along behind. My resistance to connectivity could be an indication that I'm antisocial—it's been suggested—or perhaps I'm a throwback to Ben and Clara's day, a time of Kodaks and letter-writing. Maybe it's a writer thing, but whatever the explanation, I crave periods of disconnectedness; time to be alone with my thoughts; time for wondering and imagining. Such times are needed, I believe, to bring sharper focus and create lasting images. Think of them as Kodak moments.

CHAPTER 17

THE ONLY CATHOLIC ON THE LAKE

Monday Eve—June 14th

Dearest Clara,

Certainly had fast service on your last letter from Oslo that you wrote on Thursday the 10th. It arrived here Saturday the 12th. I had gone out to the lake in the morning and Gunder brought it out that afternoon. You seem to be having a good time with your relatives, and from the sound of your letters you must eat frequently. Harold Bordewich was asking me the other day if you had seen Odd and to let him know if you did see him. Guess you didn't as I take it from you letter that you saw the younger brother. Take it from your letter that you must be a little homesick. We miss you awfully here too, but it won't be much longer now so have a good time and the time will eventually pass. Does seem like an awfully long time since you left.

Haven't been doing much since I wrote you except working. The place at home doesn't look too good and guess it has been rather neglected. The lawn does look pretty good, however. Some of the bushes around the front of the house are dead so got busy tonight and cleared out the dead stuff. The vines on the house are also dead so pulled down a bunch of them tonight. Guess I will send Emil down in the morning to clear off the rest of it and haul it out. The garden isn't of much account, and the sweet peas look rather sick. Still terribly dry and the corn fields certainly don't look very good.

Had a quiet weekend at the lake. Hardly anyone out there. Hoaglunds were out and had some company, as also were Neil Wagemakers and Russells. Guess I told you in my last letter that Neil had bought the Bunker lot. He has it all cleaned up and already has an outhouse and an old chicken coop out there. Would think he would feel rather out of place as I believe he is the only Catholic on the lake. He had also taken down the fence that we put up and moved it to the west of his lot, which makes it still better. Guess Schullers are at the North Shore and won't be out for a while. Andersons weren't out either. Guess they aren't too crazy about the lake according to some reports. Didn't do a whole lot of work this week as there was no lawn to mow. Did manage, however, to chop down a bunch of weeds on the outside of the fence along the road. Went out and tried fishing three or four hours but got nothing but bullheads. Guess fishing can't be too good as you don't see too many boats out. Will be glad when you get back to spend the weekends out there. Had a card from Ella saying they had decided to go to Michigan and not come to Minnesota for which I am glad since I had written her that we couldn't very well let our cottage go.

Charles is busy painting the woodwork in their house. They said they might be out to the lake Sunday, but Charles painted all day. Guess they have the upstairs about done and expect the paperhangers anytime. They went to Willmar tonight as Fritzie had seen something over there that she wanted to show Charles. She was over there Saturday to get some shoes for Chuckie.

Guess I sort of got mistaken in your itinerary. Thought you would be at Oslo from June 9th to the 19th, but according to your letter you were leaving there and would be traveling around Norway. I wrote you on the 10th in care of your cousin Christine so s'pose you won't get that until you reach London. I will send this letter there (London) and hope that you have better luck in getting it than the last letter I sent there. Will write you again later in the week which I hope will be in London when you get there. S'pose that will have to be my last letter. Be sure to write me or wire me the train you will arrive home on so I can be in the city to meet you. We are all fine except that we all miss you, so hurry home as fast as you can. Hope the boat trip will be more agreeable than on the way over. Your letters are very interesting and I can picture you in the things you have been doing and seeing.

I still wake up in the morning and look over at your bed and am surprised that you aren't there. Will be so glad when you are there in the morning again. Am loving you and thinking of you all the time. Had expected to get this letter off earlier today but got tied up. It's now 10:00 o'clock so time to get to bed. S'pose it is still light where you are. Take good care of yourself and remember that I love you.

All my love, Ben

It's quite likely, dear reader, that Ben and Clara have written things that piqued your interest, things that I then failed to address when it came to be my turn to write. Mostly I've skipped over the mundane and repetitive—I grew weary of outhouses and cottage windows early on—but admittedly I've also skipped over some rather crusty utterances, usually Ben's, that you might have thought worthy of further comment. Ben's remark about Neil Wagemaker being the only Catholic on the lake is a study in crustiness, and while I'd just as soon take a pass on it, I won't, though I'll address it with renewed appreciation for outhouses and windows.

The obvious question is what possible relevance does a person's religion have to where he chooses to buy lake property? After all, it's only a lake. It ain't holy water. The answer, of course, is that attitudes about such things were different in 1948. There are a couple ways to look at this. First, the big picture: there is no denying that a strain on anti-Catholicism extends back through American history, all the way to the founding days. Over the years the strain became less virulent, but in 1960, twelve years after Ben wrote his comment, John Kennedy's Catholicism was still deemed an important issue in that year's presidential election.

For our purposes, though, I hope to illuminate Ben's comment with a more local light, portraying it as the sort of tribalism small towns are prone to. That tribalism was wonderfully depicted by Jon Hassler in *Grand Opening,* a novel set in a small Minnesota town in the 1940s. Catholics patronized the Catholic grocer, while Protestants shopped the Protestant one. A fellow might well have been a Ford or a Chevy man, but that choice could well have been influenced as much by the dealer's religion as by the car itself. People wanted to associate with their own kind, and the church one attended was often a strong factor in defining "their own kind."

In many ways that tribalism was as much social as it was religious, and that puts a different light on Ben's remark, for he was no zealot. He didn't wear his religion on his sleeve. My only recollection of him saying anything that was remotely religious was to complain about the length of a sermon. He was indeed a very casual Methodist who thought the lake in summertime the better place to be on Sunday morning. In a sense, Ben's view of Catholics was the same sort of profiling he usually reserved for Democrats.

Human institutions, whether religious or social, are necessary to civilized life. They serve as anchors. They lend structure to our lives, but if the structures wall us off too completely from other cultures or ethnicities or beliefs, then our lives are diminished by them. Olivia was a more structured place in 1948. It was also very white. It took on a slight brown tinge in summer when Latino migrants came north to work the fields. Some were Mexicans, though many were U.S. citizens from southwestern states, but that distinction was rarely made by the locals. They were all called Mexicans, and come fall they were expected to leave before Minnesota turned cold and white again with the snow of winter. Over the years the demographics of the town have changed. Olivia now has a growing year-round population of folks who also happen to be Latino or black or other ethnicities. We aren't as diverse as a large city, but we're a good deal more diverse than we were, and we're better for it. It's helped maintain our population when many small towns are shrinking, and perhaps more important, diversity vitalizes our community life. Diversity means change, and change rarely comes easily, but for a town where Protestants and Catholics looked upon each other with wary eyes just sixty-some years ago, we haven't done too badly.

A discussion of religious intolerance in America wouldn't be complete without a mention of anti-Semitism, and while anti-Semitism wasn't rampant in Olivia in 1948, that was more likely due to a lack of Jews than an abundance of tolerance. I can tell you that Ben and Clara rented a modest villa in a small Pompano Beach, Florida, resort for many winters. A discreet plaque next to the office door advised potential renters that only gentiles were welcome. That said, I hasten to add that I can't recall either of them making anti-Semitic remarks any more than I can recall hearing anti-Catholic ones. Then, too, there was

Charlie Fist, the aforementioned majority owner of the Olivia Canning Company. Charlie was a Jew. And theirs was more than just a collegial business relationship. They were friends. Ben and Clara socialized with the Fists and often visited their home on Lake Minnetonka. So why even bring up anti-Semitism and that odious plaque in Florida? Good question. The answer, I think, is that it's necessary to fully understand the trajectory of tolerance. To know where we're heading, we need to know more than where we are at the moment. We also need to know from where we've come, and the path connecting then with now optimistically tells me that we're heading in the right direction. Many barriers have fallen, be they religious or racial or ethnic or gender. That immoral plaque in Florida is now illegal. But many barriers still remain, and the speed with which we tear them down is too slow for many, yet too fast for others. I fear it will always be so: ever moving in the right direction, but never quite getting to the place we ought to be.

A final note on the Big Kandiyohi Lake neighborhood: Neil Wagemaker enjoyed many happy years on the lake. His son eventually took ownership of the family cabin; then a few years ago he replaced it with a new, larger one. Their roots are deep at the lake and they make for good neighbors. Over the years we've had the pleasure of watching their family grow, and now, like us, they are visited there by grandkids. What's more, they are people of impeccable taste—they read my books and claim to like them. From time to time we socialize and get together for drinks, and when we do the conversation might go just about anywhere, but never, in my recollection, to religion.

CHAPTER 18

NEBRASKA WORDSMITHS

Monday, June 21

Dearest Ben,

We're back in London again, and so glad to be on our way home. Got in this afternoon and was so happy to have two letters waiting for me—your letter written Thursday surely made good time. It makes you seem closer to have news of you so fast. I called the other hotel to see if your first letter had come yet, and if they had forwarded it to Oslo, and they said they had returned it to you, so if you get it keep it for me, as I must have it. I got all the letters you sent to Oslo, as Christine forwarded them to me. You've been so good to write me so often. It has been so wonderful to get your letters, and to know all that you are doing. I've been so lonesome for you. This will be the last letter I'll write, and of course can't expect any more from you. Can't tell just when we will get in. We are to sail about noon Wed. and are s'posed to dock in Montreal the following Wed. but I guess they can't tell just when they will dock. There will be a railroad man on board who will make our reservations for us when they find out when we dock. We are hoping to get out of Montreal Wed. night, and maybe home by Friday. I will wire you from Chicago as to when we get in, so you had better check at the depot so as to be sure to get the wire. Now that we are on the way home we can hardly wait. I wish we were flying home.

I think it would be nice to have Shirley and Bob home for the Fourth. I shouldn't be too tired after a week on the boat, and if they are there for just the weekend it shouldn't be too bad. So let's have them come, don't you think?

Weekends especially I've thot of you at the lake and wished so I could be there too. Am glad Jacobsons are finally getting at their cottage. Too bad Andersons are disappointed.

Friday after I wrote you we took a ride out into the country to the church where my mother attended and where my grandparents are buried—a very nice church, pipe organ and all. Then we stopped at Christine's home—where they live when her husband doesn't have to be in Oslo for the Storthing. Their son is living there now; it's a lovely home with beautiful gardens. Of course we ate there. I forgot that about noon we went to call on some folks—the lady had been one of my mother's pupils—so we had lunch there and lunch after we got home. Seems like every time we turn around we eat. Agnes, my cousin, certainly feeds us well. Such good food, and everything served so beautifully. That night we went to dinner at a 2nd cousin's—a lovely home and a good time. Relatives were there too. Most talk a little English so we get along fine. Leo said if he were there long enuf, he'd be talking Norwegian. By the way, I've had quite a bit of lobster. That's all to the good for me. Sat. morning we went to call on another sweet old lady who had been one of my mother's pupils. Then after lunch we took a taxi to town where we were to catch the boat for Stavanger. Agnes went with us. It was about a 45 minute ride, but not very fast as the road was narrow and winding. We had a fine boat ride, about 1½ hours. At Stavanger we walked around and visited the old Dom Kircke—800 years old—a wedding was in progress so we took that in too. We wandered all over town, had some supper, then went to the dock as they said our boat for London might be in by 9 o'clock. However, it was late and we waited around till 12 before it came, so by the time we got on board and thru customs it was 1 o'clock. I went right to bed and to sleep. When I woke up about 9 o'clock the boat was rolling quite a bit. The North Sea isn't supposed to be very calm. I decided to stay in bed, as I felt so much better there. Bertha stayed in bed all day too as she was sick. I had lunch and dinner in bed, and tho I didn't eat very much, I didn't lose it. I slept most of the time so it wasn't too bad. The boat docked about 3 this morning, but we stayed in bed until 6, so had a good night's sleep. We got right on the boat train which left at 8:50 and got here about 4. We got registered, then walked up to Piccadilly and had dinner at Scotto and went to a movie after and then back to the hotel. Big Ben just struck midnight so I will go to bed and finish this before we leave London. Good night, my dear.

Tuesday eve: Just got thru dinner here at the hotel, am going to finish this letter, take a bath and to bed. It is 8:30, but we've had a full day, and want to get up in the morning as our boat train leaves at 9:40. This morning we walked to Buckingham Palace and saw the changing of the guard—quite a colorful sight. After lunch we went on a tour out to Windsor Castle, and enjoyed that so much. We drove thru a lot of lovely countryside, stopped at Eaton; saw the lads in their long striped trousers, cut-aways and high silk hats. We visited the church at Stoke Pages, where Grey wrote his elegy.

We wandered all thru the grounds at Windsor Castle. Then we went to Hampton Court, an old castle belonging to Henry VIII. The gardens there were beautiful, as William of Orange started to copy the gardens at Versailles. Our guide reminded me so of Bob, in looks, his smile, his ways and his build. He took us in the Underground to meet the sightseeing bus, so we got to see where so many Londoners slept during the war.

We have done so much, seen so much, I suppose I will forget a lot, but it really has been a wonderful trip, except that I have been so lonely for you all the time. Tis wonderful to know that you are loving me and missing me too. You are the best husband in the world. I love you so and can hardly wait to get home.

All my love, Clara

Once again we have an opportunity to compare twenty-first century connectivity with that of 1948. In Ben's previous letter he encouraged Clara to write or wire him her arrival time in Minneapolis so that he could be there to meet the train. Now Clara, writing from London, points to the difficulty in knowing just when the ship will dock in Montreal, and the resulting uncertainty as to which train she will be on. She advises that she will wire Ben from Chicago and that he should check at the depot for the wire. The depot she referred to wasn't the train station in Minneapolis. It was the railroad depot in Olivia, a humble wooden structure alongside the tracks, similar to the ones in every other town along the line. In 1948 each of those depots was manned by an agent who conducted the railroad's business and who also was trained to send and receive Morse code with a telegraph key. Today an arrival time can be sent quickly by means of a cell phone call, or worse, a text. While news arriving, clicking and clacking, over the singing telegraph wires may be slower, it is far more elegant, at least to a romantic like me.

This letter of Clara's from London is her last, and Ben's letter following this one will be his last; once again, the letters are out of sequence. Wanting to be sure that Clara would get his letter, Ben mailed it on June 17. Apparently mail service between Olivia and London was quicker than between Olivia and continental Europe, as Clara actually received his last letter before writing her own on June 21. I again considered switching the order, but then decided, no; the letters have alternated throughout the book and there's no point in changing at the very end. However, I will offer one clarification for you, dear reader. In Clara's letter she seems to be selling Ben on the idea that Shirley and Bob, my aunt and uncle from Nebraska, should come to the lake for the Fourth of July. She argues that after a week on the ship she will be well rested and up to having company. In Ben's letter we will see why Clara resorted to salesmanship, as he fusses that she will arrive home tired and suggests that he write Shirley and tell her not to come. I don't doubt that Ben worried about Clara needing rest after her long journey, but I suspect there was more to his plan than that. Recall from an earlier chapter that the lake was Ben's querencia, that special harbor where he found peace and contentment. His letters have consistently revealed that his contentment grows as the number of people at the lake declines, but that doesn't apply to Clara. She's part of his querencia; she adds to it. Their letters are replete with their longing for one another, and they often cite the lake as the place where they most long to be together. Sure, Ben worried about Clara getting overly tired, but I also think he was looking forward to some one-on-one time with his wife at his querencia.

We don't know whether the Nebraskans came north for that Fourth of July or not; the letters don't say, but I'd bet that they did. As much as Clara looked forward to being with Ben at the lake, she also loved being surrounded by family, especially on holidays. Shirley and

Bob rarely missed a holiday with the family. For the Fourth of July we would gather at the lake, of course, but on Thanksgiving and Christmas and Easter the venue was usually Ben and Clara's stucco house where we would squeeze around a big oak table in the dining room for our holiday feasts. As noted before, love came out of Clara's kitchen, and never more so than on those holidays. Later, after my family had moved into the stucco house and Clara was no longer up to all that cooking, it became my mother's turn, but regardless of who the cook was, the fare was always exceptional. And on those special occasions there was invariably something else served up along with the food, something to add spice and flavor to the meal: the English language.

FAMILY AND FRIENDS GATHER AROUND THE DINING ROOM TABLE IN THE STUCCO HOUSE FOR GOOD FOOD AND CONVERSATION.

The King's English was spoken in my home. My parents had a strong command of the language, and that allowed Judy and me to gain our own command in the best way: early and at home. But when the Nebraska wordsmiths arrived, language rose to a different level. Shirley and Bob ran a small-town newspaper, and they did it well, garnering numerous awards. They were people who made their living writing sentences and paragraphs, a tedious task to some, but a joyous one for my aunt and uncle, and that joy would spill over our holiday table. The conversation would quickly soar past the mundane. Small talk never had a chance against the playful repartee and banter that echoed around the table. I remember those meals as times when I began to realize how much fun can be had with language, the joy that can be found in the simple act of stringing together words.

CHAPTER 19

HEROES

Thursday, June 17th

Dearest Clara,

Have been holding off until I got another letter from you before writing but if this is to reach you in London, guess I had better get it off as the first letter I wrote you there didn't make very good time. I guess this will have to be the last letter unless they can reach you on the boat. Four weeks ago today I put you on the train and it seems like four months. Two more weeks and you should be aboard the train for home and will we all be glad to see you. Thought I would have another letter from you before this, but you must be either busy moving around so much or didn't get the connections that your last letter got. That certainly came thru in a hurry.

Haven't done much since writing you on Monday. Went out to men's nite at the club Tues. but couldn't get better than a 43. Guess my golf isn't so good any more. Didn't have too much of a crowd out. Served hamburger and onion sandwiches, also potato chips and pickles. Tasted good. Have also been trying to get some work done around the yard. The vines on the house and porch all died again, so cleaned that up. Also some of the bushes around the house that had died out. Have been thinking of fixing up the window boxes, but don't know just what to get. We are getting a nice rain today. Has been raining slowly all morning, which is just what we need. Will take a lot of it. We were out looking at some of the corn and it was beginning to show the effects of the drought. If this keeps up we won't have to worry about whether we get any Mexicans, corn picking machines or anything else.

Charles is still busy at their house. Guess he hasn't spent any time at the plant for the last 10 days. He is painting, and of course isn't too fast at it. They have one bedroom papered, so should be thru with papering in the next day or two. Then they have to sand the floors so they may still be in our house when you get back. Has been nice to have them there and it has also been nice for them to have a nice place to live in while they had all that mess. Guess he is beginning to find out what things really cost when you begin to remodel.

Charles wants to take the pickup to the city with him this weekend when he goes in to fly. Said they had some stuff at Taylors that he wanted to bring home. Guess Taylors are moving to Iowa shortly. Jacobsons finally found a couple of carpenters and they are to be there tomorrow to run the foundation. George and I are going out tonight and stay over while the foundation is being run. Gunder said he might go along too as he thought it would be fun to watch it. Hope George can cook, though I suppose I will have to do most of that. Will have to be back in here tomorrow nite as I am taking the pickup out and Charles wants it for Saturday morning.

Last week Fritzie said she and the kids were going out to the lake with me for the weekend since Charles would be gone. Don't s'pose she will want to go if it keeps on raining. Will be so glad when you get back to spend the weekends at the lake. Am enclosing another letter from Shirley. Think I will write and tell her they hadn't better plan on coming up here for the 4th. You will just have gotten home and I think it will be better if they come after you have rested up some. Didn't do any good to have them here right after getting back from Florida.

Went to the movies last night. "Two Suns" or some such name. Fritzie said it was s'posed to be so good, but wasn't too impressed. They are working on the curb and gutter in front of our place now. Have the apron to the alley all cemented so can't drive in there. Have to come up the back way. They took out that big box elder of Schamber's. Didn't put in our walk, so don't know when we will get it. Marian is home with her two kids. Chuckie was out in the yard pushing one of them around yesterday. Said he didn't like her. Fritzie has been busy making curtains and what not. I think their house is going to look pretty good when they get it fixed up. Will have so much money in it, however, that they will have to stay there.

Hope you have a better crossing coming home and that you will enjoy the boat. Will see you at the train in about two weeks. Be sure to wire me as to when you will get in, or if you know now maybe you will write the time of arrival. Will be so glad to see you and have you home again. Has been too long a time, hasn't it? Am loving you and thinking of you all the time. Told Harold about your meeting his cousin. Take good care of yourself and come home fast.

All my love, Ben

It's Ben's last letter and he's clearly happy that his wife will soon return and that my family will soon move out of his home and into our own. He takes a final shot at my dad's slow painting and lavish remodeling. I don't envy the carpenters who would run the foundation for Jacobson's cottage, what with Ben Brown and George Jacobson and Gunder Hoaglund overseeing. I have no recollection of pushing a little girl around the yard, but then I was only two. I suppose it was so, but my manners have markedly improved since, and I've also acquired a much higher opinion of the opposite sex.

Ben's mention of my dad going into the city to fly refers to his continuing service in the Navy Reserve. For seven years after the war he would spend one weekend a month flying out of the naval air station at Wold-Chamberlain Field, now known as the Minneapolis-St. Paul International Airport.

In a right world every boy's first hero would be his father. Mine made that easy, despite being a slow painter. He was Hollywood handsome, and in addition to his athletic prowess already noted, he was a member of the 1936 University of Minnesota national championship football team. But it was his service as a Navy pilot in the South Pacific during World War II that most thrilled my boy heart.

As mentioned earlier, he was already in the Navy and undergoing flight training when the Japanese struck Pearl Harbor. He completed his training early in March of 1942 and was assigned to a squadron of PBY Catalinas, the twin-engine patrol bomber that was also a seaplane. His war then paused for a quick trip to Minnesota where he married his high school sweetheart in a hastily arranged ceremony. He and my mother then drove to San Francisco where they enjoyed a few days of honeymooning before Dad reported for duty. His squadron left for Hawaii and Mother went to San Diego, where she would stay with her sister Irene and her brother-in-law Bill, who worked at an aircraft factory there.

By mid-April Dad's squadron, VP12, was flying twelve-hour patrols out of Kaneohe Bay Naval Air Station on the island of Oahu.

On June 3 they flew one of those long patrols probing for the Japanese fleet that Naval intelligence was expecting to strike Midway Island. They didn't find the ships, but the next day the Japanese had drawn closer and other PBYs spotted them. The Battle of Midway, one of the war's most decisive, followed.

A note here to explain how I can say with precision when he flew and for how long. I have his aviator's flight logs, which document in pilot-speak the date, duration, and purpose of every flight he made for the Navy from 1941 through 1952. They start with him flying open-cockpit biplane trainers and end with the logging of his 3,261st hour. I treasure them as if he had written them for me.

A Navy PBY Catalina.

After the Battle of Midway the squadron continued patrol flights out of Kaneohe until mid-July, at which time they moved to Midway where they operated for the next several months. Then in November of 1942 they headed south and west, stopping off at different American bases on their way to the Solomon Islands and Guadalcanal, the focal point of the war in the Pacific at the time. That transit to Guadalcanal involved a story that Dad loved to tell. On November 25 they arrived in Samoa. The next day would be Thanksgiving and turkey with all the trimmings was on the menu, but that day they dined on beans and franks. The next morning they took off before dinner was served for a six-hour flight to Fiji, where they hoped to enjoy their Thanksgiving meal. Unfortunately, in flying to Fiji they also crossed the international date line, so upon landing it was the day after Thanksgiving. Turkey had been served the day before and that day's menu was, you guessed it, beans and franks.

The Marines had only recently secured Guadalcanal, and in doing so they captured the airfield the Japanese had been building there at the time. It was renamed Henderson Field, and Navy and Marine planes were soon operating from it. VP12 was the first squadron of PBYs at Henderson, and their arrival prompted the question as to how best to use them.

The PBY was a very versatile airplane. It could land on the water, making it useful for sea rescue operations, but the model flown by VP12 had retractable landing gear so it could take off and land on runways as well. It could stay in the air for many hours, making it an ideal plane for long-range patrols. It could drop bombs and torpedoes and even depth charges in anti-submarine missions. Its chief drawback was that it was slow, and therefore no match for fast and highly maneuverable enemy fighter planes. That deficiency was addressed by shortening "Catalina" to "Cat" and painting the planes black. VP12 then became creatures of the night, the first Black Cat Squadron.

They would take off from Henderson at dusk, not to return until dawn. Under cover of darkness, they would attack enemy ships coming down The Slot, as the north-south sound separating the Solomon Islands was called. They also bombed enemy bases and airfields in the northern Solomons. A highly effective tactic was for the planes to drop flares near enemy ships, thereby illuminating them for the guns of our warships. VP12 operated in this manner from Henderson Field on Guadalcanal for over six months, and when they were finally relieved they had earned a Presidential Unit Citation.

THE SECRETARY OF THE NAVY
WASHINGTON

The President of the United States takes pleasure in presenting the PRESIDENTIAL UNIT CITATION to

PATROL SQUADRON TWELVE

for service as set forth in the following

CITATION:

"For extraordinary heroism in action against enemy Japanese forces during operations in the South Pacific War Area, from November 24, 1942, to June 1, 1943. The first Catalina squadron to operate from Guadalcanal and the originator of the highly effective night tactics peculiar to 'Black Cats', Patrol Squadron TWELVE pioneered this type of aerial warfare during the critical months when our position in this area was still uncertain. Flying at low altitudes, frequently in the face of concentrated antiaircraft fire and hazardous weather, the Squadron overcame all obstacles in conducting night searches and anti-submarine missions, night spotting for cruiser task forces, and night torpedo, bombing and harrassing missions. With only nine planes available for operations and with a lack of spare parts and personnel to repair these aircraft, the Squadron struck the enemy at every opportunity and, by its skillful and aggressive tactics, inflicted damage on important enemy shore installations at Munda, Villa Plantation, Buka and Kahili, and on Japanese shipping in the Solomon Islands Area. Outstanding for its indomitable fighting spirit, Patrol Squadron TWELVE established a standard for subsequent Catalina squadrons and achieved a gallant record of service which reflects the highest credit upon its pilots and crews and the United States Naval Service."

For the President,

James Forrestal

Secretary of the Navy

The squadron then rotated back to the States, to San Diego, having been deployed in the Pacific for over fourteen months. Duty in San Diego consisted of patrols and training, and there was also time for rest and recreation, some of that recreation resulting in my sister. Then after only six months in San Diego, it was back to the South Pacific and the war zone for another nine-month deployment. By the time that was over, Dad had been awarded the Air Medal three times.

THE PILOTS OF VP12 ON GUADALCANAL.
CHARLES BROWN IS FIRST ON THE LEFT, TOP ROW.

His final months of the war were spent in Cocoa Beach, Florida, where he was reunited with his wife and the daughter who had been born while he was away. He was stationed at the nearby Banana River Naval Air Station, a federal facility better known today as Cape Canaveral and the Kennedy Space Center. His flying time was again taken up with patrols and training, and there was once more the opportunity for rest and recreation. I was born in February of 1946, so it's a matter of simple arithmetic to determine that Cocoa Beach was the place of my conception, though given the proximity to Canaveral I prefer to think of it as my launching.

In the summer of 1945 the possibility of a third deployment to the Pacific loomed large as the anticipated invasion of Japan was expected to be long and bloody. Hiroshima and Nagasaki changed that, and by the end of September he had returned to Minnesota and civilian life.

I have one vivid recollection from my dad's postwar years flying with the reserve. I was perhaps four or five years old. It was a Saturday in summertime. After supper Mother hustled Judy and me through our baths and into our pajamas and robes, then herded us out to the front lawn at dusk. Something was up, but she wouldn't say what. A surprise. We waited in the fading light; then came the sound of approaching aircraft. We looked to the western sky and saw three PBYs flying in formation at no more than 3,000 feet. When they were directly overhead, one of the planes peeled from formation and flew a tight circle above our house as the pilot's children leaped with joy below.

Bert Blyleven was a Hall of Fame pitcher for the Minnesota Twins. Now in retirement, he does color commentary on televised Twins games. During lulls in the baseball action he often uses something called a telestrator to circle various fans in the stands. For their part, the fans vie for this attention by holding up signs imploring, "Circle me, Bert!" It's an obvious thrill to be circled by a Hall of Famer. I can understand that, having once been circled by my own hero.

EPILOGUE

Clara made it safely home; we moved into our newly remodeled house; life returned to normal. The summer of 1948 remained dry, though rain came in August. Crops were harvested and the Olivia Canning Company had a packing season.

The late Bill Holm wrote affectionately of his hometown and the people who lived there in *The Heart Can Be Filled Anywhere on Earth: Minneota, Minnesota*. In that book he relates that Flannery O'Connor was asked her opinion of some new school of fashionable novelists. She responded by saying, "You know what's the matter with them? They're not from anywhere." Bill went on to write eloquently of what he chose to call *from-ness* and its importance to a complete life, that life without *from-ness* is too often hollow. As a rule we don't get to choose where we are from, but that makes it no less crucial to a filled heart.

Letters from the Attic is my book about *from-ness*. It's about the place and the people I am from, the place and people I love. Love is remarkable in its ability to grow, even in harsh conditions, but it grows best when rooted in *from-ness*. And my sense of *from-ness* has grown with the writing. Ben and Clara and my parents were people I thought I knew well, but writing about them has taken that knowledge to a new level. To think about someone, to remember them, is one thing; to write about them is quite another.

Writing is a revealing process. Invariably, I have discovered things by the end of a work that I didn't know at the start. It may just be facts and figures that were needed to tell the story, but often it's more than that, often it's a hard-to-define sense of having grown closer to something or someone. At the start I knew that I would relate family history and anecdotes. I would touch on the history of Olivia, Minnesota. I knew that I would strive to amuse at every opportunity and that I would climb on soapboxes and speak my mind. What I didn't know at the start, what I know now, is the extent to which I would speak my heart.